MW00355922

FREE DVD   **FREE**   FREE DVD

From Stress to Success DVD from Trivium Test Prep

Dear Customer,

Thank you for purchasing from Trivium Test Prep! Whether you're looking to join the military, get into college, or advance your career, we're honored to be a part of your journey.

To show our appreciation (and to help you relieve a little of that test-prep stress), we're offering a **FREE *OAR Essential Test Tips DVD*** by Trivium Test Prep. Our DVD includes 35 test preparation strategies that will help keep you calm and collected before and during your big exam. All we ask is that you email us your feedback and describe your experience with our product. Amazing, awful, or just so-so: we want to hear what you have to say!

To receive your **FREE *OAR Essential Test Tips DVD***, please email us at 5star@triviumtestprep.com. Include "Free 5 Star" in the subject line and the following information in your email:

1. The title of the product you purchased.
2. Your rating from 1 – 5 (with 5 being the best).
3. Your feedback about the product, including how our materials helped you meet your goals and ways in which we can improve our products.
4. Your full name and shipping address so we can send your **FREE *OAR Essential Test Tips DVD***.

If you have any questions or concerns please feel free to contact us directly at 5star@triviumtestprep.com.

Thank you, and good luck with your studies!

OAR PRACTICE BOOK:

Practice Test Questions for the
Officer Aptitude Rating Exam

Elissa Simon

TABLE OF CONTENTS

INTRODUCTION

Congratulations on choosing to test for your Officer Aptitude Rating (OAR)! By purchasing this book, you've taken an important step on your path to joining the military.

This guide will provide you with a detailed overview of the OAR, so you know exactly what to expect on exam day. We'll take you through all the concepts covered on the exam and give you the opportunity to test your knowledge with practice questions. Even if it's been a while since you last took a major exam, don't worry; we'll make sure you're more than ready!

WHAT ARE THE ASTB-E AND THE OAR?

The Officer Aptitude Rating (OAR) is a portion of the larger Aviation Selection Test Battery (ASTB-E) test. The ASTB-E measures candidate's verbal and quantitative ability, mechanical understanding, spatial awareness, and knowledge of general aviation concepts. The OAR includes only the portions of the ASTB-E that cover verbal and quantitative abilities and mechanical understanding.

Which Scores are Included in the OAR?

SUBTEST	OAR	ASTB-E
Math Skills	X	X
Reading Comprehension	X	X
Mechanical Comprehension	X	X
Aviation and Nautical Information		X
Naval Aviation Trait Facet Inventory		X
Performance Based Measures Battery		X
Biographical Inventory with Response Validation		X

The ASTB-E is used to determine eligibility of college graduates desiring to become an aviation officer (pilot and first officer) in the US Navy, Marine Corps, or Coast Guard. Individuals applying for nonaviation officer programs, such as Officer Candidate School (OCS), may only be required to take the OAR portions of the test.

The ASTB-E is developed and monitored by the Naval Operational Medicine Institute (NOMI). The Educational Testing Service collaborated with NOMI to produce the exam in paper and computer adaptive test formats. The Naval Personnel Command and Commandant of the Marine Corps establish eligibility requirements.

The ASTB-E is administered at Navy Recruiting Districts (NRDs), Navy ROTC units at selected universities, and Marine Corps Officer Selection Offices (OSOs). High school candidates applying for the navy and coast guard military academies or NROTC and college graduates with a bachelor degree are eligible academically to take the exam.

COMPUTER ADAPTIVE TESTING

Computer adaptive testing (CAT) allows the test administrators to get a more complete view of your skills in less time and with fewer questions. These tests start with a question of average difficulty. If you answer this question correctly, the next question will be harder; if you answer it incorrectly, the next question will be easier. This continues as you go through the section, with questions getting harder or easier based on how well you perform. Once you've answered enough questions for the computer to determine your score, that section of the test will end.

Often you will be able to immediately see your score after taking a CAT exam. You will also probably answer fewer questions than if you'd taken a paper-and-pencil test, and each section will take less time. However, you will not be able to go back and check or change your answers.

The ASTB-E is offered in both CAT and paper-and-pencil form.

WHAT'S ON THE OAR?

The ASTB-E, revised in 2013, has three versions—Form 6, Form 7, and Form 8. Previous versions (Form 1 through Form 5) are no longer being used, although test scores are still valid provided the applicant has not retaken the exam with Form 6 through Form 8.

The current ASTB-E has seven subtest components. Candidates seeking nonaviation positions are only required to take the Math, Reading, and Mechanical Tests to obtain their OAR.

The individual ASTB-E subtests included in the OAR are

- Math Skills Test (MST)
- Reading Skills Test (RST)
- Mechanical Comprehension Test (MCT)

The OAR portion of the ASTB-E is offered in paper format and CAT format. The paper format requires strict time limits for subtests, whereas the time taken for each subtest in the CAT format may be shortened. Since, the computer automatically provides harder or easier questions depending on the correctness of the candidate's answers, actual test-taking time is adjusted on the CAT.

What's on the OAR?

SUBTEST	NUMBER OF QUESTIONS (PAPER)	NUMBER OF QUESTIONS (CAT)	TIME LIMIT
Math Skills Test	30	20 – 30	40 minutes
Reading Skills Test	20	20 – 30	30 minutes
Mechanical Comprehension Test	30	20 – 30	15 minutes
Total	80 questions	60 – 90 questions	Up to

Breakdown of the Subtests

- **Math Skills Test (MST)**—requires you to solve for algebraic, arithmetic, and geometric equations and word problems. Questions may include formulas, probability, fractions, ratios, and time and distance estimations.
- **Reading Skills Test (RST)**—evaluates your reading comprehension by interpreting word passages.
- **Mechanical Comprehension Test (MCT)**—measures your understanding of high school-level physics problems. These problems may include questions about gases and liquids, pulleys, fulcrums, pressure, volume, velocity, principles of electricity, weight distribution, and performance of engines.

How Is the OAR Scored?

The ASTB-E paper exam is sent back to NOMI for scoring. Unlike other military aptitude tests, recruiters are not provided an unofficial score and must wait for the official score. The ASTB-E CAT exam is scored immediately after completing the exam.

Nonaviation candidates who only take the OAR portion of the ASTB-E will receive one rating as the OAR. Scores are ranked from 20 to 80 based on three subtests (MST, RST, and MCT). For current minimum score eligibility requirements, contact your recruiter or refer to the Navy Personnel Command Program Authorizations 106 and 107 and Marine Corps Order 1542.11.

RETAKING THE OAR

There is a three-time lifetime limit to attempt the ASTB-E. If a candidate wishes to retest, the date of retest must be no earlier than thirty-one days after the date the initial exam was taken. If a second retest is desired, the candidate may retest not earlier than ninety-one days after first retest.

Exam results of candidates who previously took the ASTB-E (Form 1 through Form 5) do not count toward the three-time lifetime limit; however, those results remain valid until another ASTB-E is taken.

Individuals who took the ASTB-E for an OAR only may return within thirty days of the initial test to complete the ASTB-E by taking the remaining subtests. This is called a *test merge*. In this case, candidates must wait until the OAR score is received prior to taking the remaining subtests. Additionally, even if the OAR portion was taken by paper format, the remaining test must be conducted using the CAT format. The date the candidate completes the remaining subtests is considered the official test date toward the three-time lifetime limit.

For example, Candidate Doe takes an initial ASTB-E for an OAR on March 1. He decides to take the remaining subtests for eligibility toward an aviation position. He has until March 31 of the same year to finish the complete ASTB-E. His first official test date toward his three-time lifetime limit is now March 31 (or any date beforehand) when he completed all subtests of the ASTB-E. If Candidate Doe never returned before March 31 to take the remaining subtests, his first official test date remains as March 1 and counts toward his three-time lifetime limit.

HOW IS THE OAR ADMINISTERED?

If you are ready to take the OAR portion of the ASTB-E, contact your local recruiter. Your recruiter will determine your initial qualifications and schedule you to take the ASTB-E. The location where you take the ASTB-E will be decided when a test seat is available. Possible testing locations include Navy recruiting stations, NROTC units at selected universities, Marine Corps officer selection offices, and military institutes.

On the day of the exam, you will need to bring an identification card and your Social Security card to verify your identity. Testing materials are provided by the test proctor. Calculators are not allowed. If your recruiter drives you to the testing location, the recruiter cannot be in the testing room. Personal breaks are scheduled by the proctor, so be prepared to remain in the testing seat until dismissed.

GETTING TO KNOW THE UNITED STATES MILITARY

The US Navy is tasked with missions to maintain freedom on the seas and in the sky above the seas. The US Navy has enlisted personnel, warrant officers, and commissioned officers among its ranks. Navy officers are listed in three categories:

- junior officer (includes ranks of O-1 to O-4)—ensign, lieutenant junior grade, lieutenant, and lieutenant commander
- senior officer (includes ranks of O-5 and O-6)—commander and captain
- flag officer (includes ranks of O-7 to O-10)—rear admiral lower half, rear admiral, vice admiral, and admiral

The US Navy offers officer career fields in surface warfare, submarine, aerospace maintenance, chaplaincy, healthcare, supply, logistics, and transportation as well as aviation positions as a naval aviator and flight officer.

The US Coast Guard's role is to protect the public, environment, and US economic interests at the nation's ports, waterways, international waters, and maritime regions necessary to protect national security. The Coast Guard's officer ranks match those of the US Navy. They also have enlisted personnel and warrant officers. The Coast Guard offers commissioning career fields in law; the US Public Health Service; aviation; engineering; command, control, and communications; computer technologies; and intelligence.

The US Marine Corps is designed and trained for offensive amphibious employments and as an expeditionary force in readiness for multinational military operations. The Marine Corps officer ranks match those of the US Army:

- company-grade officer—second lieutenant, first lieutenant, and captain
- field-grade officer—major, lieutenant colonel, and colonel
- general officer—brigadier general, major general, lieutenant general, and general

The Marine Corps offers officer career fields in personnel, administration, intelligence, infantry, Marine Air-Ground Task Force plans, communications, field artillery, and training.

THE MILITARY RECRUITMENT PROCESS

As stated before, the OAR is just one requirement toward qualification for military service as an officer in the US Navy, Marine Corps, or Coast Guard. You may contact your local recruiter through your high school counselor or college adviser, or visit your local military recruitment center.

Once you contact your local recruiter, he or she will meet with you at the recruiting office, your school, or your home. During this meeting, the recruiter will conduct an interview to initiate the recruitment process. This process begins with the recruiter determining if you meet the basic qualification requirements. Expect a review of your education level, financial record, background investigation, interests, criminal record or drug history, height and weight, age, and citizenship.

Once basic qualifications have been established, the recruiter refers you to an officer recruiter who will schedule you to take the ASTB-E. Once receiving your official scores, your recruiter will schedule you for a physical exam. You will meet with your officer recruiter to discuss your OAR scores and any medical issue that may preclude your entrance to an officer commissioning school leading to an appointment as an officer. During this meeting, the officer recruiter will discuss which branch(es) of service you qualify for and possible career options for you to choose from. Your recruiter can answer any concerns or questions you have along the way.

ABOUT THIS GUIDE

This guide will help you master the most important test topics and also develop critical test-taking skills. We have built features into our books to prepare you for your tests and increase your score. Along with a detailed summary of the test's format, content, and scoring, we offer an in-depth overview of the content knowledge required to pass the test. In the review you'll find sidebars that provide interesting information, highlight key concepts, and review content so that you can solidify your understanding of the exam's concepts. You can also test your knowledge with sample questions throughout the text and practice questions that reflect the content and format of the OAR portion of the ASTB-E. We're pleased you've chosen Trivium Test Prep to be a part of your military journey!

PRACTICE TEST ONE

MATH SKILLS

40 minutes

This section measures your knowledge of mathematical terms and principles. Each question is followed by four possible answers. You are to decide which one of the four choices is correct.

1. Simplify: $-(3^2) + (5 - 7)^2 - 3(4 - 8)$
   - (A) −17
   - (B) −1
   - (C) 7
   - (D) 25

2. If a person reads 40 pages in 45 minutes, approximately how many minutes will it take her to read 265 pages?
   - (A) 202
   - (B) 236
   - (C) 265
   - (D) 298

3. W, X, Y, and Z lie on a circle with center A. If the diameter of the circle is 75, what is the sum of $\overline{AW}$, $\overline{AX}$, $\overline{AY}$, and $\overline{AZ}$?
   - (A) 75
   - (B) 300
   - (C) 150
   - (D) 106.5

4. A worker was paid $15,036 for 7 months of work. If he received the same amount each month, how much was he paid for the first 2 months?
   - (A) $2,148
   - (B) $4,296
   - (C) $6,444
   - (D) $8,592

5. 40% of what number is equal to 17?
   - (A) 2.35
   - (B) 6.8
   - (C) 42.5
   - (D) 680

6. The measures of two angles of a triangle are 25° and 110°. What is the measure of the third angle?
   - (A) 40°
   - (B) 45°
   - (C) 50°
   - (D) 55°

7. Michael is making cupcakes. He plans to give $\frac{1}{2}$ of the cupcakes to a friend and $\frac{1}{3}$ of the cupcakes to his coworkers. If he makes 48 cupcakes, how many will he have left over?

(A) 8

(B) 10

(C) 16

(D) 24

8. Which of the following is closest in value to 129,113 + 34,602?

(A) 162,000

(B) 163,000

(C) 164,000

(D) 165,000

9. If $j = 4$, what is the value of $2(j - 4)^4 - j + \frac{1}{2}j$?

(A) 0

(B) −2

(C) 2

(D) 4

10. Which of the following is equivalent to $(5^2 - 2)^2 + 3^3$?

(A) 25

(B) 30

(C) 556

(D) 538

11. In the fall, 425 students pass the math benchmark. In the spring, 680 students pass the same benchmark. What is the percentage increase in passing scores from fall to spring?

(A) 37.5%

(B) 55%

(C) 60%

(D) 62.5%

12. What is the area of the shape?

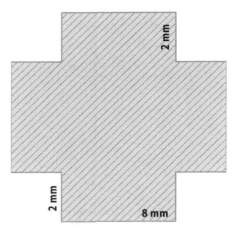

(A) 6 mm²

(B) 16 mm²

(C) 64 mm²

(D) 128 mm²

13. A fruit stand sells apples, bananas, and oranges at a ratio of 3:2:1. If the fruit stand sells 20 bananas, how many total pieces of fruit does the fruit stand sell?

(A) 10

(B) 30

(C) 40

(D) 60

14. Erica is at work for $8\frac{1}{2}$ hours a day. If she takes one 30-minute lunch break and two 15-minute breaks during the day, how many hours does she work?

(A) 6 hours, 30 minutes

(B) 6 hours, 45 minutes

(C) 7 hours, 15 minutes

(D) 7 hours, 30 minutes

15. If the value of y is between 0.0047 and 0.0162, which of the following could be the value of y?

(A) 0.0035

(B) 0.0055

(C) 0.0185

(D) 0.0238

16. A car traveled at 65 miles per hour for $1\frac{1}{2}$ hours and then traveled at 50 miles per hour for $2\frac{1}{2}$ hours. How many miles did the car travel?

(A) 190.5 miles

(B) 215.0 miles

(C) 222.5 miles

(D) 237.5 miles

17. A bike store is having a 30%-off sale, and one of the bikes is on sale for $385. What was the original price of this bike?

(A) $253.00

(B) $450.00

(C) $500.50

(D) $550.00

18. Adam is painting the outside walls of a 4-walled shed. The shed is 5 feet wide, 4 feet deep, and 7 feet high. How many square feet of paint will Adam need?

(A) 46 square feet

(B) 63 square feet

(C) 126 square feet

(D) 140 square feet

19. A grocery store sold 30% of its pears and had 455 pears remaining. How many pears did the grocery store start with?

(A) 602

(B) 650

(C) 692

(D) 700

20. A landscaping company charges 5 cents per square foot for fertilizer. How much would they charge to fertilize a 30-foot-by-50-foot lawn?

(A) $7.50

(B) $15.00

(C) $75.00

(D) $150.00

21. What is the value of the expression $0.5^x + 1$ when $x = -2$?

(A) 0.75

(B) 1.25

(C) 4

(D) 5

22. John and Ethan are working at a car wash. It takes John 1 hour to wash 3 cars. Ethan can wash 3 cars in 45 minutes. If they work together, how many cars can they wash in 1 hour?

(A) 6

(B) 7

(C) 9

(D) 12

23. Tiles are $12.51 per square yard. What will it cost to cover the floor of a room with tiles if the room is 10 feet wide and 12 feet long?

(A) $166.80

(B) $178.70

(C) $184.60

(D) $190.90

24. How many digits are in the sum $951.4 + 98.908 + 1.053$?

(A) 4

(B) 5

(C) 6

(D) 7

25. Melissa is ordering fencing to enclose a square area of 5,625 square feet. How many feet of fencing does she need?

(A) 75 feet

(B) 150 feet

(C) 300 feet

(D) 5,625 feet

READING COMPREHENSION

30 minutes

This section measures your ability to read and understand written material. Passages are followed by a series of multiple-choice questions. You are to choose the option that best answers the question based on the passage. No additional information or specific knowledge is needed.

The Battle of Little Bighorn, commonly called Custer's Last Stand, was a battle between the Lakota, the Northern Cheyenne, the Arapaho, and the Seventh Calvary Regiment of the US Army. Led by war leaders Crazy Horse and Chief Gall and the religious leader Sitting Bull, the allied tribes of the Plains Indians decisively defeated their US foes. Two hundred and sixty-eight US soldiers were killed, including General George Armstrong Custer, two of his brothers, his nephew, his brother-in-law, and six Indian scouts.

1. What is the main idea of this passage?

   (A) Most of General Custer's family died in the Battle of Little Bighorn.

   (B) The Seventh Calvary regiment was formed to fight Native American tribes.

   (C) Sitting Bull and George Custer were fierce enemies.

   (D) The Battle of Little Bighorn was a significant victory for the Plains Indians.

In 1953, doctors surgically removed the hippocampus of patient Henry Molaison in an attempt to stop his frequent seizures. Unexpectedly, he lost the ability to form new memories, leading to the biggest breakthrough in the science of memory. Molaison's long-term memory—of events more than a year before his surgery—was unchanged as was his ability to learn physical skills. From this, scientists learned that different types of memory are handled by different parts of the brain, with the hippocampus responsible for *episodic memory,* the short-term recall of events. They have since discovered that some memories are then channeled to the cortex, the outer layers of the brain that handle higher functions, where they are gradually integrated with related information to build lasting knowledge about our world.

2. The main idea of the passage is that

   (A) Molaison's surgery posed significant risk to the functioning of his brain.

   (B) short-term and long-term memory are stored in different parts of the brain.

   (C) long-term memory forms over a longer period than short-term memory.

   (D) memories of physical skills are processed differently than memories of events.

Archaeologists have discovered the oldest known specimens of bedbugs in a cave in Oregon where humans once lived. The three different species date back to between 5,000 and 11,000 years ago. The finding gives scientists a clue as to how bedbugs became human parasites. These bedbugs, like those that plague humans today, originated as bat parasites. Scientists hypothesize that it was the co-habitation of humans and bats in the caves that encouraged the bugs to begin feeding on the humans. The three species found in the Oregon caves are actually still around today, although they continue to prefer bats. Humans only lived seasonally in the Oregon cave system, however, which might explain why these insects did not fully transfer to human hosts like bedbugs elsewhere did.

3. With which of the following claims about bedbugs would the author most likely agree?

   (A) Modern bedbugs that prefer humans thrive better in areas with extensive light.

   (B) Bedbugs are a relatively fragile species that has struggled to survive over time.

   (C) The transition to humans significantly accelerated the growth of bedbug populations.

   (D) Bedbugs that prefer humans originated in caves that humans occupied year-round.

The Bastille, Paris's famous historical prison, was originally built in 1370 as a fortification, called a *bastide* in Old French, to protect the city from English invasion during the Hundred Years' War. It rose 100 feet into the air, had eight towers, and was surrounded by a moat more than eighty feet wide. In the seventeenth century, the government converted the fortress into an elite prison for upper-class felons, political disruptors, and spies. Residents of the Bastille arrived by direct order of the king and usually were left there to languish without a trial.

4. In the first sentence, the word *fortification* most nearly means

   (A) royal castle.

   (B) national symbol.

   (C) seat of government.

   (D) defensive structure.

Taking a person's temperature is one of the most basic and common health care tasks. Everyone from nurses to emergency medical technicians to concerned parents should be able to grab a thermometer to take a patient or loved one's temperature. But what's the best way to get an accurate reading? The answer depends on the situation.

The most common way people measure body temperature is orally. A simple digital or disposable thermometer is placed under the tongue for a few minutes, and the task is done. There are many situations, however, when measuring temperature orally isn't an option. For example, when a person can't breathe through his nose, he won't be able to keep his mouth closed long enough to get an accurate reading. In these situations, it's often preferable to place the thermometer in the rectum or armpit. Using the rectum also has the added benefit of providing a much more accurate reading than other locations can provide.

It's also often the case that certain people, like agitated patients or fussy babies, won't be able to sit still long enough for an accurate reading. In these situations, it's best to use a thermometer that works much more quickly, such as one that measures temperature in the ear or at the temporal artery. No matter which method is chosen, however, it's important to check the average temperature for each region, as it can vary by several degrees.

5. Which statement is NOT a detail from the passage?

   (A) Taking a temperature in the ear or at the temporal artery is more accurate than taking it orally.

   (B) If an individual cannot breathe through the nose, taking his or her temperature orally will likely give an inaccurate reading.

   (C) The standard human body temperature varies depending on whether it's measured in the mouth, rectum, armpit, ear, or temporal artery.

   (D) The most common way to measure temperature is by placing a thermometer in the mouth.

6. What is the author's primary purpose in writing this essay?

(A) to advocate for the use of thermometers that measure temperature in the ear or at the temporal artery

(B) to explain the methods available to measure a person's temperature and the situation where each method is appropriate

(C) to warn readers that the average temperature of the human body varies by region

(D) to discuss how nurses use different types of thermometers depending on the type of patient they are examining

7. What is the meaning of the word *agitated* in the last paragraph?

(A) obviously upset

(B) quickly moving

(C) violently ill

(D) slightly dirty

8. According to the passage, why is it sometimes preferable to take a person's temperature rectally?

(A) Rectal readings are more accurate than oral readings.

(B) Many people cannot sit still long enough to have their temperatures taken orally.

(C) Temperature readings can vary widely between regions of the body.

(D) Many people do not have access to quick-acting thermometers.

One of the most dramatic acts of nonviolent resistance in India's movement for independence from Britain came in 1930, when independence leader Mahatma Gandhi organized a 240-mile march to the Arabian Sea. The goal of the march was to make salt from seawater, in defiance of British law. The British prohibited Indians from collecting or selling salt—a vital part of the Indian diet—requiring them instead to buy it from British merchants and pay a heavy salt tax. The crowd of marchers grew along the way to tens of thousands of people. In Dandi, Gandhi picked up a small chunk of salt and broke British law. Thousands in Dandi followed his lead as did millions of fellow protestors in coastal towns throughout India. In an attempt to quell the civil disobedience, authorities arrested more than 60,000 people across the country, including Gandhi himself.

9. With which of the following claims about civil disobedience would the author most likely agree?

(A) Civil disobedience is a disorganized form of protest easily quashed by government.

(B) Civil disobedience requires extreme violations of existing law to be effective.

(C) Civil disobedience is an effective strategy for effecting political change.

(D) Civil disobedience is only effective in countries that already have democracy.

The odds of success for any new restaurant are slim. Competition in the city is fierce, and the low margin of return means that aspiring restaurateurs must be exact and ruthless with their budget and pricing. The fact that The City Café has lasted as long as it has is a testament to its owners' skills.

10. Which of the following conclusions is well supported by the passage?
   (A) The City Café offers the best casual dining in town.
   (B) The City Café has a well-managed budget and prices items on its menu appropriately.
   (C) The popularity of The City Café will likely fall as new restaurants open in the city.
   (D) The City Café has a larger margin of return than other restaurants in the city.

11. Which of the following is the meaning of *testament* as used in the last sentence?
   (A) story
   (B) surprise
   (C) artifact
   (D) evidence

We've been told for years that the recipe for weight loss is fewer calories in than calories out. In other words, eat less and exercise more, and your body will take care of the rest. As many of those who've tried to diet can attest, this edict doesn't always produce results. If you're one of those folks, you might have felt that you just weren't doing it right—that the failure was all your fault.

However, several new studies released this year have suggested that it might not be your fault at all. For example, a study of people who'd lost a high percentage of their body weight (>17%) in a short period of time found that they could not physically maintain their new weight. Scientists measured their resting metabolic rate and found that they'd need to consume only a few hundred calories a day to meet their metabolic needs. Basically, their bodies were in starvation mode and seemed to desperately hang on to each and every calorie. Eating even a single healthy, well-balanced meal a day would cause these subjects to start packing back on the pounds.

Other studies have shown that factors like intestinal bacteria, distribution of body fat, and hormone levels can affect the manner in which our bodies process calories. There's also the fact that it's actually quite difficult to measure the number of calories consumed during a particular meal and the number used while exercising.

12. Which of the following would be the best summary statement to conclude the passage?
   (A) It turns out that conventional dieting wisdom doesn't capture the whole picture of how our bodies function.
   (B) Still, counting calories and tracking exercise is a good idea if you want to lose weight.
   (C) In conclusion, it's important to lose weight responsibly: losing too much weight at once can negatively impact the body.
   (D) It's easy to see that diets don't work, so we should focus less on weight loss and more on overall health.

13. Which of the following would weaken the author's argument?

   (A) a new diet pill from a pharmaceutical company that promises to help patients lose weight by changing intestinal bacteria

   (B) the personal experience of a man who was able to lose a significant amount of weight by taking in fewer calories than he used

   (C) a study showing that people in different geographic locations lose different amounts of weight when on the same diet

   (D) a study showing that people often misreport their food intake when part of a scientific study on weight loss

When a fire destroyed San Francisco's American Indian Center in October of 1969, American Indian groups set their sights on the recently closed island prison of Alcatraz as a site of a new Indian cultural center and school. Ignored by the government, an activist group known as Indians of All Tribes sailed to Alcatraz in the early morning hours with eighty-nine men, women, and children. They landed on Alcatraz, claiming it for all the tribes of North America. Their demands were ignored, and so the group continued to occupy the island for the next nineteen months, its numbers swelling up to 600 as others joined. By January of 1970, many of the original protestors had left, and on June 11, 1971, federal marshals forcibly removed the last residents.

14. The main idea of this passage is that

   (A) the government refused to listen to the demands of American Indians.

   (B) American Indians occupied Alcatraz in protest of government policy.

   (C) few people joined the occupation of Alcatraz, weakening its effectiveness.

   (D) the government took violent action against protestors at Alcatraz.

In an effort to increase women's presence in government, several countries in Latin America, including Argentina, Brazil, and Mexico, have implemented legislated candidate quotas. These quotas require that at least 30 percent of a party's candidate list in any election cycle consists of women who have a legitimate chance at election. As a result, Latin America has the greatest number of female heads of government in the world, and the second highest percentage of female members of parliament after Nordic Europe. However, these trends do not carry over outside of politics. While 25 percent of legislators in Latin America are now women, less than 2 percent of CEOs in the region are female.

15. What is the main idea of the passage?

   (A) In Latin America, political parties must nominate women for office.

   (B) Latin America is the region with the greatest gender equality.

   (C) Women in Latin America have greater economic influence than political influence.

   (D) Women have a significant presence in Latin American politics.

Tourists flock to Yellowstone National Park each year to view the geysers that bubble and erupt throughout it. What most of these tourists do not know is that these geysers are formed by a caldera, a hot crater in the earth's crust, that was created by a series of three eruptions of an ancient supervolcano. These eruptions, which began 2.1 million years ago, spewed between 1,000 to 2,450 cubic kilometers of volcanic matter at such a rate that the volcano's magma chamber collapsed, creating the craters.

16. The main idea of the passage is that
   (A) Yellowstone National Park is a popular tourist destination.
   (B) The geysers in Yellowstone National Park rest on a caldera in the earth's crust.
   (C) A supervolcano once sat in the area covered by Yellowstone National Park.
   (D) The earth's crust is weaker in Yellowstone National Park.

When the Spanish-American War broke out in 1898, the US Army was small and understaffed. President William McKinley called for 1,250 volunteers primarily from the Southwest to serve in the First US Volunteer Calvary. Eager to fight, the ranks were quickly filled by a diverse group of cowboys, gold prospectors, hunters, gamblers, Native Americans, veterans, police officers, and college students looking for an adventure. The officer corps was composed of veterans of the Civil War and the Indian Wars. With more volunteers than it could accept, the army set high standards: all the recruits had to be skilled on horseback and with guns. Consequently, they became known as the Rough Riders.

17. According to the passage, all the recruits were required to
   (A) have previously fought in a war.
   (B) be American citizens.
   (C) live in the Southwest.
   (D) ride a horse well.

At first glance, the landscape of the northern end of the Rift Valley appears to be a stretch of barren land. Paleoanthropologists, however, have discovered an abundance of fossils just beneath the dusty surface. They believe this area once contained open grasslands near lakes and rivers, populated with grazing animals. Forty miles from this spot, in 1974, scientists uncovered a 3.2 million-year-old non-human hominid they nicknamed "Lucy." And, in 2013, researchers found the oldest fossil in the human ancestral line. Before this, the oldest fossil from the genus *Homo*—of which *Homo sapiens* are the only remaining species—dated only back to 2.3 million years ago, leaving a 700,000-year gap between Lucy's species and the advent of humans. The new fossil dated back to 2.75 and 2.8 million years ago, pushing the appearance of humans back 400,000 years.

18. According to the passage, the discovery of Lucy
   (A) gave scientists new information about the development of humans.
   (B) provided evidence of a different ecosystem in the ancient Rift Valley.
   (C) supported the belief that other hominids existed significantly before humans.
   (D) closed the gap between the development of other hominids and humans.

CONTINUE

The social and political discourse of America continues to be permeated with idealism. An idealistic viewpoint asserts that the ideals of freedom, equality, justice, and human dignity are the truths that Americans must continue to aspire to. Idealists argue that truth is what should be, not necessarily what is. In general, they work to improve things and to make them as close to ideal as possible.

19. Which of the following best captures the author's purpose?

(A) to advocate for freedom, equality, justice, and human rights

(B) to explain what an idealist believes in

(C) to explain what's wrong with social and political discourse in America

(D) to persuade readers to believe in certain truths

Alexander Hamilton and James Madison called for the Constitutional Convention to write a constitution as the foundation of a stronger federal government. Madison and other Federalists like John Adams believed in separation of powers, republicanism, and a strong federal government. Despite the separation of powers that would be provided for in the US Constitution, anti-Federalists like Thomas Jefferson called for even more limitations on the power of the federal government.

20. In the context of the passage below, which of the following would most likely NOT support a strong federal government?

(A) Alexander Hamilton

(B) James Madison

(C) John Adams

(D) Thomas Jefferson

The cisco, a foot-long freshwater fish native to the Great Lakes, once thrived throughout the basin but had virtually disappeared by the 1950s. However, today fishermen are pulling them up by the net-load in Lake Michigan and Lake Ontario. It is highly unusual for a native species to revive, and the reason for the cisco's reemergence is even more unlikely. The cisco have an invasive species, quagga mussels, to thank for their return. Quagga mussels depleted nutrients in the lakes, harming other species highly dependent on these nutrients. Cisco, however, thrive in low-nutrient environments. As other species—many invasive—diminished, cisco flourished in their place.

21. It can be inferred from the passage that most invasive species

(A) support the growth of native species.

(B) do not impact the development of native species.

(C) struggle to survive in their new environments.

(D) cause the decline of native species.

After looking at five houses, Robert and I have decided to buy the one on Forest Road. The first two homes we visited didn't have the space we need—the first had only one bathroom, and the second did not have a guest bedroom. The third house, on Pine Street, had enough space inside but didn't have a big enough yard for our three dogs. The fourth house we looked at, on Rice Avenue, was stunning but well above our price range. The last home, on Forest Road, wasn't in the neighborhood we wanted to live in. However, it had the right amount of space for the right price.

22. What is the author's conclusion about the house on Pine Street?
   (A) The house did not have enough bedrooms.
   (B) The house did not have a big enough yard.
   (C) The house was not in the right neighborhood.
   (D) The house was too expensive.

It could be said that the great battle between the North and South we call the Civil War was a battle for individual identity. The states of the South had their own culture, one based on farming, independence, and the rights of both man and state to determine their own paths. Similarly, the North had forged its own identity as a center of centralized commerce and manufacturing. This clash of lifestyles was bound to create tension, and this tension was bound to lead to war. But people who try to sell you this narrative are wrong. The Civil War was not a battle of cultural identities—it was a battle about slavery. All other explanations for the war are either a direct consequence of the South's desire for wealth at the expense of her fellow man or a fanciful invention to cover up this sad portion of our nation's history. And it cannot be denied that this time in our past was very sad indeed.

23. What is the meaning of the word *fanciful* in the passage?
   (A) complicated
   (B) imaginative
   (C) successful
   (D) unfortunate

24. What is the author's primary purpose in writing this essay?
   (A) to convince readers that slavery was the main cause of the Civil War
   (B) to illustrate the cultural differences between the North and the South before the Civil War
   (C) to persuade readers that the North deserved to win the Civil War
   (D) to demonstrate that the history of the Civil War is too complicated to be understood clearly

The greatest changes in sensory, motor, and perceptual development happen in the first two years of life. When babies are first born, most of their senses operate in a similar way to those of adults. For example, babies are able to hear before they are born; studies show that babies turn toward the sound of their mothers' voices just minutes after being born, indicating they recognize the mother's voice from their time in the womb.

The exception to this rule is vision. A baby's vision changes significantly in its first year of life; initially it has a range of vision of only 8 – 12 inches and no depth perception. As a result, infants rely primarily on hearing; vision does not become the dominant sense until around the age of 12 months. Babies also prefer faces to other objects. This preference, along with their limited vision range, means that their sight is initially focused on their caregiver.

25. Which of the following senses do babies primarily rely on?
   (A) vision
   (B) hearing
   (C) touch
   (D) smell

MECHANICAL COMPREHENSION

15 minutes

This section measures your understanding of basic mechanical principles. Each question is followed by three possible answers. You are to decide which one of the three choices is correct.

1.
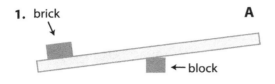

Compared to figure A above, the brick in figure B will

(A) be lifted the same height, and it will take the same amount of effort to do so.

(B) be lifted higher, and it will take more effort to do so.

(C) not be lifted as high, and it will take more effort to do so.

2. Because a crowbar has a fulcrum in the middle of the effort and the resistance, it is an example of a

(A) first-class lever.

(B) second-class lever.

(C) third-class lever.

3.
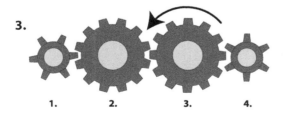

Which of the other gears is moving in the same direction as Gear 3?

(A) Gear 1 only

(B) Gear 2 only

(C) Gear 4 only

4.
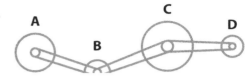

If Pulley B is the driver and turns clockwise, which pulley turns the slowest?

(A) Pulley A turns the slowest.

(B) Pulley C turns the slowest.

(C) Pulley D turns the slowest.

5.
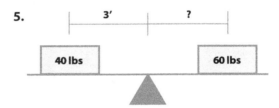

A 40-pound block and a 60-pound block are placed on a uniform board as shown above. How far to the right of the fulcrum must the 60-pound block be placed in order for the board to be balanced?

(A) 1 foot

(B) 2 feet

(C) 4 feet

6.

The simple machine shown above is an example of

(A) a lever.

(B) a pulley.

(C) an inclined plane.

7.

pulley

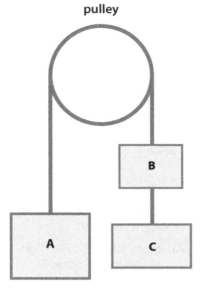

Blocks A, B, and C are hanging from a pulley as shown in the figure. If Block A weighs 70 pounds and Block B weighs 20 pounds, what must the weight of Block C be in order for the blocks to be at rest?

(A) 30 pounds

(B) 35 pounds

(C) 50 pounds

8.

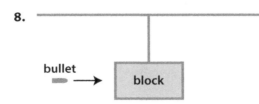

A bullet is shot at a stationary block that is hanging from the ceiling as shown. What direction will the block swing after the bullet hits the block?

(A) down and to the right

(B) down and to the left

(C) up and to the right

9. Why is it so difficult to hold a beach ball under water?

(A) The ball is full of air, which is much less dense than water.

(B) The ball expands under water, so it rises faster.

(C) The cool water will cool the air in the ball, making it rise.

10.

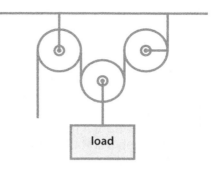

A block is hanging from a pulley system as shown in the figure. The theoretical mechanical advantage of the system is

(A) 1.

(B) 2.

(C) 3.

11. On Earth, Objects A and B have the same mass and weight. If Object B is moved to the moon, which of the following statements is true?

(A) Both objects have the same mass, but Object A now has the greater weight.

(B) Both objects have the same weight, but Object A now has the greater mass.

(C) Both objects still have the same mass and weight.

12.

An object is being carried by three people as shown above. Which person bears the most weight?

(A) A

(B) B and C

(C) All three bear the same weight.

→ CONTINUE

13.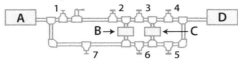

open to air

In the figure shown below, assume that all valves are closed. For the air to flow from A to D without flowing through B and C, it is necessary to open valves

(A) 1, 2, and 5.

(B) 1, 2, 3, and 4.

(C) 5, 6, and 7.

14. A steel ball with a temperature of 150°C is dropped into a liquid with a temperature of 120°C. Which of the following statements about the equilibrium temperature has to be true?

(A) The equilibrium temperature is exactly 135°C.

(B) The equilibrium temperature is between 120°C and 150°C.

(C) The equilibrium temperature is exactly 270°C.

15. Water is flowing through Pipe A, which has a diameter of 15 cm, into Pipe B, which has a diameter of 20 cm. The water will flow

(A) faster through Pipe A.

(B) faster through Pipe B.

(C) at the same speed through Pipe A and Pipe B.

16. Water flows out of a water tower at a rate of 3 gallons per minute and flows in at a rate of 140 gallons per hour. After one hour, the volume of water in the tank will be

(A) the same.

(B) 40 gallons less.

(C) 40 gallons more.

17.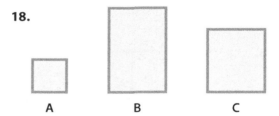

Scale A   Scale B

A weight is placed on a uniform board between two identical scales. Which of the following statements is true?

(A) Scale A will show a higher reading than Scale B because more weight is to the left of the fulcrum.

(B) Scale B will show a higher reading than Scale A because more weight is to the left of the fulcrum.

(C) The scales read the same weight.

18.

A   B   C

The three containers shown above are filled with the same gas. Which statement is true?

(A) Container A will experience the greatest pressure.

(B) Container B will experience the greatest pressure.

(C) Container C will experience the greatest pressure.

19. Two charges are held at a distance of 1 m from each other. Charge q_1 is −2e and charge q_2 is −2e. What will happen when the charges are released and free to move?

(A) q_1 and q_2 will remain at rest and not move.

(B) q_1 and q_2 will attract and move closer together.

(C) q_1 and q_2 will repel and move farther apart.

20.

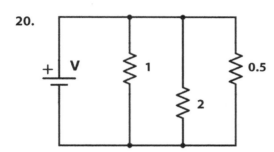

Find the equivalent resistance, R_{eq}, for the circuit in the figure above.

(A) 0.5 kΩ

(B) 1 kΩ

(C) 3.5 kΩ

21. What is the key electrical difference between a conducting material and an insulating material?

(A) A conducting material will conduct electricity, and an insulating material will not.

(B) A conducting material creates electrons, and an insulating material destroys them.

(C) An insulating material will create heat when electricity flows through it, and a conducting material will not.

22. An 80-pound object is placed on a scale inside an elevator that begins to travel upward. The scale will read that the weight of the object is

(A) 80 pounds.

(B) greater than 80 pounds.

(C) less than 80 pounds.

23. Two ropes are connected on either side of a mass of 100 kg resting on a flat surface. Each rope is pulling on the mass with 50 N of force, parallel to the ground. What can be said about the motion of the mass?

(A) The mass will accelerate to left.

(B) The mass is in equilibrium.

(C) The mass will accelerate to the right.

24.

A   B

Objects A and B have the same mass and are placed in separate graduated cylinders that are each filled with 50 mL of water. If the water level rises higher in the cylinder containing Object B, which statement is true?

(A) Object A has a higher density than Object B.

(B) Object B has a higher density than Object A.

(C) Objects A and B have the same density.

25. A boat is crossing a river with a fast-moving current. If the captain aims the boat at a point of the opposite bank directly across from his starting point, where will the boat land?

(A) Downstream from his starting point

(B) Upstream from his starting point

(C) Directly across from his starting point

ANSWER KEY

MATH SKILLS

1. **(C)**

   Simplify using PEMDAS.
   $$-(3^2) + (5 - 7)^2 - 3(4 - 8)$$
   $$= -(3^2) + (-2)^2 - 3(-4)$$
   $$= -9 + 4 - 3(-4)$$
   $$= -9 + 4 + 12 = \mathbf{7}$$

2. **(D)**

   Write a proportion and then solve for x.
   $$\frac{40}{45} = \frac{265}{x}$$
   $$40x = 11{,}925$$
   $$x = 298.125 \approx \mathbf{298}$$

3. **(C)**

   All the points lie on the circle, so each line segment is a radius. The sum of the 4 lines will be 4 times the radius.
   $$r = \frac{75}{2} = 37.5$$
   $$4r = \mathbf{150}$$

4. **(B)**

   Write a proportion and then solve for x.
   $$\frac{15{,}036}{7} = \frac{x}{2}$$
   $$7x = 30{,}072$$
   $$x = \mathbf{4{,}296}$$

5. **(C)**

   Use the equation for percentages.
   $$whole = \frac{part}{percentage} = \frac{17}{0.4} = \mathbf{42.5}$$

6. **(B)**

   The sum of the measures of the three angles in a triangle is 180°. Subtract the two given angle measures from 180 to find the measure of the third angle.
   $$180° - 25° - 110° = \mathbf{45°}$$

7. **(A)**

   Add the number of cupcakes he will give to his friend and to his coworkers, then subtract that value from 48.
   # of cupcakes for his friend:
   $$\frac{1}{2} \times 48 = 24$$
   # of cupcakes for his coworkers:
   $$\frac{1}{3} \times 48 = 16$$
   $$48 - (24 + 16) = \mathbf{8}$$

8. **(C)**

   Round each value and add.
   $$129{,}113 \approx 129{,}000$$
   $$34{,}602 \approx 35{,}000$$
   $$129{,}000 + 35{,}000 = \mathbf{164{,}000}$$

9. (B)

Plug 4 in for j and simplify.

$2(j-4)^4 - j + \frac{1}{2}j$

$2(4-4)^4 - 4 + \frac{1}{2}(4) = \mathbf{-2}$

10. (C)

Simplify using PEMDAS.

$(5^2 - 2)^2 + 3^3$

$(25 - 2)^2 + 3^3$

$(23)^2 + 3^3$

$529 + 27 = \mathbf{556}$

11. (C)

Use the formula for percent change.

$percent\ change = \frac{amount\ of\ change}{original\ amount}$

$= \frac{(680 - 425)}{425}$

$= \frac{255}{425} = 0.60 = \mathbf{60\%}$

12. (D)

Find the area of the square as if it did not have the corners cut out.

$12\ mm \times 12\ mm = 144\ mm^2$

Find the area of the four cut out corners.

$2\ mm \times 2\ mm = 4\ mm^2$

$4(4\ mm^2) = 16\ mm^2$

Subtract the area of the cut out corners from the large square to find the area of the shape.

$144\ mm^2 - 16\ mm^2 = \mathbf{128\ mm^2}$

13. (D)

Assign variables and write the ratios as fractions. Then, cross multiply to solve for the number of apples and oranges sold.

x = apples

$\frac{apples}{bananas} = \frac{3}{2} = \frac{x}{20}$

$60 = 2x$

$x = 30$ apples

y = oranges

$\frac{oranges}{bananas} = \frac{1}{2} = \frac{y}{20}$

$2y = 20$

$y = 10$ oranges

To find the total, add the number of apples, oranges, and bananas

together. $30 + 20 + 10 = \mathbf{60\ pieces}$ **of fruit**

14. (D)

Find the time that Erica spends on break and subtract this from her total time at work.

$30 + 2(15) = 1$ hour

$8\frac{1}{2} - 1 = 7\frac{1}{2} = \mathbf{7\ hours,\ 30\ minutes}$

15. (B)

All of the decimal numbers are expressed in ten-thousandths. 55 is between 47 and 162, so **0.0055** is between 0.0047 and 0.0162.

16. (C)

Multiply the car's speed by the time traveled to find the distance.

$1.5(65) = 97.5$ miles

$2.5(50) = 125$ miles

$97.5 + 125 = \mathbf{222.5\ miles}$

17. (D)

Set up an equation. The original price (p) minus 30% of the original price is $385.

$p - 0.3p = 385$

$p = \frac{385}{0.7} = \mathbf{\$550}$

18. (C)

Two of the walls are 5 feet by 7 feet. The other two walls are 4 feet by 7 feet. Therefore, the total area of the four walls is:

$2(5)(7) + 2(4)(7) = 70 + 56 =$ **126 square feet**

19. (B)

Set up an equation. If p is the original number of pears, the store has sold $0.30p$ pears. The original number minus the number sold will equal 455.

$p - 0.30p = 455$

$p = \frac{455}{0.7} = \mathbf{650\ pears}$

20. (C)

Multiply the area by the charge per square foot.

Area = 50 × 30 = 1,500 square feet
1,500 × 0.05 = **$75.00**

21. (D)

Substitute −2 for x and evaluate.
$0.5^{-2} + 1 = 4 + 1 = $ **5**

22. (B)

Use a proportion to find the number of cars that Ethan can wash in 1 hour (60 minutes). Then add to answer the question.

$\frac{3}{45} = \frac{x}{60}$

$3(60) = x(45)$

$180 = 45x$

$4 = x$

$3 + 4 = $ **7**

23. (A)

Find the area of the room in square feet and convert it to square yards (1 square yard = 9 square feet). Then multiply by the cost per square yard.

Area = 10 × 12 = 120 square feet

$\frac{120}{9} = \frac{40}{3}$ square yards

$\frac{40}{3} \times \$12.51 = \frac{\$500.40}{3} = $ **$166.80**

24. (D)

Add zeros as needed so that each number is expressed in thousandths; then add the numbers.
951.400 + 98.908 + 1.053 =
1,051.361 → **7 digits**

25. (C)

Use the area to find the length of a side of the square. Then find the perimeter of the square.

$x^2 = 5,625$

$x = \sqrt{5,625} = 75$

Perimeter = $4x = 4(75) = $ **300 feet**

1. (A) is incorrect. While the text does list several family members of Custer who died in the battle, this is not the main idea.

   (B) is incorrect. The author does not explain why the cavalry was formed.

   (C) is incorrect. The author does not describe the personal relationship between Sitting Bull and Custer.

   (D) is correct. The author writes, "the allied tribes…decisively defeated their US foes."

2. (A) is incorrect. While the author does describe his memory loss, this is not the main idea of the passage.

   (B) is correct. The author writes, "From this, scientists learned that different types of memory are handled by different parts of the brain."

   (C) is incorrect. The author does explain the differences in long-term and short-term memory formation, but not until the end of the passage.

   (D) is incorrect. While it is implied that memories of physical skills are processed differently than memories of events, this is not the main idea of the passage.

3. (A) is incorrect. The author does not address the impact of light on bedbugs.

   (B) is incorrect. The author explains that the three discovered species still exist today.

   (C) is incorrect. The author does not address the growth rate of bedbug populations.

   (D) is correct. The author writes, "Humans only lived seasonally in the Oregon cave system, however, which might explain why these insects did not fully transfer to human hosts like bedbugs elsewhere did."

4. (A) is incorrect. There is no indication that the Bastille was occupied by royalty.

   (B) is incorrect. There is no indication that the structure was intended to represent anything.

   (C) is incorrect. There is no indication that the Bastille was used for governing.

   (D) is correct. The author writes that the Bastille was originally built "to protect the city from English invasion during the Hundred Years' War."

5. **(A) is correct.** This detail is not stated in the passage.

   (B) is incorrect. The second paragraph states that "when a person can't breathe through his nose, he won't be able to keep his mouth closed long enough to get an accurate reading."

   (C) is incorrect. The final paragraph states that "[no] matter which method [of taking a temperature] is chosen, however, it's important to check the average temperature for each region, as it can vary by several degrees."

   (D) is incorrect. The second paragraph states that "[t]he most common way people measure body temperature is orally."

6. (A) is incorrect. Thermometers that measure temperature in the ear and temporal artery are mentioned in the passage; however, they are a supporting detail for the author's primary purpose.

   (B) is correct. In the first paragraph, the author writes, "But what's the best way to get an accurate reading? The answer depends on the situation." She then goes on to describe various options and their applications.

   (C) is incorrect. Though this detail is mentioned, it is not the author's primary focus.

   (D) is incorrect. The author writes about how many people—not only nurses—use different types of thermometers in different situations.

7. **(A) is correct.** The final paragraph states that "agitated patients...won't be able to sit still long enough for an accurate reading." The reader can infer that an agitated patient is a patient who is visibly upset, annoyed, or uncomfortable.

(B) is incorrect. While some agitated patients may move quickly, this is not necessarily the meaning of the word in context.

(C) is incorrect. The term *violently ill* does not necessarily explain why a patient would have a difficult time sitting still.

(D) is incorrect. The team *slightly dirty* does not explain why a patient would have a difficult time sitting still.

8. **(A) is correct.** The second paragraph of the passage states that "[u]sing the rectum also has the added benefit of providing a much more accurate reading than other locations can provide."

(B) is incorrect. In the final paragraph, the author suggests that "certain people, like agitated patients or fussy babies" might have a difficult time sitting still but does not suggest that this is a problem for "many" people.

(C) is incorrect. In the final paragraph, the author writes that "it's important to check the average temperature for each region, as it can vary by several degrees," but does not cite this as a reason to use a rectal thermometer.

(D) is incorrect. The author does not mention access to thermometers as a consideration.

9. (A) is incorrect. The author writes that the protest spread in spite of government attempts to end it.

(B) is incorrect. The author writes, "In Dandi, Gandhi picked up a small chunk of salt and broke British law." Picking up a piece of salt is not itself an extreme act; Gandhi was able to make a big statement with a small action.

(C) is correct. The author describes a situation in which civil disobedience had an enormous impact.

(D) is incorrect. The action the author describes occurred in India when it was controlled by Britain, a colonial and nondemocratic power.

10. (A) is incorrect. The author points to the skills of the owner as the reason for The City Café's long-term success, not the quality of the dining experience.

(B) is correct. The passage states that restaurateurs must be "exact and ruthless with their budget and pricing." The success of The City Café implies that its owners have done that.

(C) is incorrect. The passage suggests that most new restaurants struggle but does not discuss how new restaurants affect the popularity of existing restaurants.

(D) is incorrect. The passage implies that all restaurateurs must work with the low margin of return and simply suggests that the owners of The City Café have made the most of it, not that they have any advantage in this respect.

11. (A) is incorrect. This answer choice does not fit in the context of the sentence; the author has not told a story about The City Café's success.

(B) is incorrect. This answer choice does not fit in the context of the sentence; the author does not indicate surprise.

(C) is incorrect. This answer choice does not fit in the context of the sentence.

(D) is correct. *Evidence* best describes the idea that The City Café's longevity is proof of its owners' skills.

12. **(A) is correct.** The bulk of the passage is dedicated to showing that conventional wisdom about "fewer calories in than calories out" isn't true for many people and is more complicated than previously believed.

(B) is incorrect. The author indicates that calorie counting is not an effective way to lose weight.

(C) is incorrect. Though the author indicates that this may be the case, the negative impacts of losing weight quickly are not the main point of the passage; a more inclusive sentence is needed to conclude the passage successfully.

(D) is incorrect. The author does not indicate that diets don't work at all, simply that the scientific understanding of dieting is still limited.

13. (A) is incorrect. A new diet pill would have no effect on the existing studies and would not prove anything about conventional dieting wisdom.

(B) is incorrect. A single anecdotal example would not be enough to contradict the results of well-designed studies; if anything, the account would provide another example of how complex the topics of dieting and weight loss are.

(C) is incorrect. This answer choice would strengthen the author's argument by highlighting the complexity of the topic of dieting.

(D) is correct. People misreporting the amount of food they ate would introduce error into studies on weight loss and might make the studies the author cites unreliable.

14. (A) is incorrect. While the author states this, it is not the main idea.

(B) is correct. The author states, "Ignored by the government, an activist group known as Indians of All Tribes sailed to Alcatraz in the early morning hours with eighty-nine men, women, and children." The author goes on to describe the nineteen-month occupation of the island.

(C) is incorrect. The author states that up to 600 people joined the occupation.

(D) is incorrect. The author does not describe any violent action towards protestors.

15. (A) is incorrect. While this fact is stated in the passage, it is not the main idea.

(B) is incorrect. The author writes, "However, these trends do not carry over outside of politics."

(C) is incorrect. The author explains that women have a large amount of political influence but less economic influence.

(D) is correct. The passage discusses the large number of women in political positions in Latin America.

16. (A) is incorrect. While this is stated in the first sentence, it is not the main idea.

(B) is correct. The passage describes the origin of Yellowstone's geysers.

(C) is incorrect. While the author states this in the passage, it is not the main idea.

(D) is incorrect. This is not stated in the passage.

17. (A) is incorrect. The author writes that the officers, not the volunteers, were veterans.

(B) is incorrect. The passage does not mention a citizenship requirement.

(C) is incorrect. While most of the volunteers were indeed from the Southwest, the passage does not say this was a requirement.

(D) is correct. The author writes, "the army set high standards: all of the recruits had to be skilled on horseback…."

18. (A) is incorrect. The author writes, "scientists uncovered a 3.2 million-year-old non-human hominid they nicknamed 'Lucy.'"

(B) is incorrect. The author does not connect Lucy's discovery with the knowledge about the area's past ecosystem.

(C) is correct. The author writes that before Lucy's discovery, the oldest known fossil from the genus Homo "dated only back to 2.3 million years ago, leaving a 700,000-year gap between Lucy's species and the advent of humans."

(D) is incorrect. The author explains it was the 2013 discovery that narrowed the gap.

19. (A) is incorrect. The author identifies the ideals associated with idealism but does not offer an opinion on or advocate for them.

(B) is correct. The purpose of the passage is to explain what an idealist believes in. The author does not offer any opinions or try to persuade readers about the importance of certain values.

(C) is incorrect. The author states that social and political discourse are "permeated with idealism" but does not suggest that this is destructive or wrong.

(D) is incorrect. The author provides the reader with information but does not seek to change the reader's opinions or behaviors.

20. (A) is incorrect. The author states that "Alexander Hamilton…called for the Constitutional Convention to write a constitution as the foundation of a stronger federal government."

(B) is incorrect. The author states that "James Madison called for the Constitutional Convention to write a constitution as the foundation of a stronger federal government."

(C) is incorrect. The author states that "Federalists like John Adams believed in… a strong federal government."

(D) is correct. In the passage, Thomas Jefferson is defined as an anti-Federalist, in contrast with Federalists who believed in a strong federal government.

21. (A) is incorrect. The author provides no evidence that invasive species typically help native species.

(B) is incorrect. The author writes that the quagga mussels, an invasive species, harmed native species.

(C) is incorrect. The author implies that quagga mussels are thriving.

(D) is correct. The author writes that "the reason for the cisco's reemergence is even more unlikely. The cisco have an invasive species, quagga mussels, to thank for their return."

22. (A) is incorrect. The author indicates that the house on Pine Street "had enough space inside[.]"

(B) is correct. The author says that the house on Pine Street "had enough space inside but didn't have a big enough yard for [their] three dogs."

(C) is incorrect. The author does not mention the neighborhood of the Pine Street house.

(D) is incorrect. The author does not mention the price of the Pine Street house.

23. (A) is incorrect. The author does not suggest that the narrative of the Civil War as "a battle for individual identity" is a complicated one, only that it is untrue.

(B) is correct. The author writes, "All other explanations for the war are either a direct consequence of the South's desire for wealth at the expense of her fellow man or a fanciful invention to cover up this sad portion of our nation's history."

(C) is incorrect. The author does not discuss the extent to which the attempt to "cover up this sad portion of our nation's history" was successful or unsuccessful.

(D) is incorrect. Though the author may agree that the invention of the identity narrative is unfortunate, this is not the best answer choice to highlight her main assertion that it is untrue.

24. **(A) is correct.** The author writes, "But people who try to sell you this narrative are wrong. The Civil War was not a battle of cultural identities—it was a battle about slavery."

(B) is incorrect. Though the author describes the cultural differences between the North and South in the first half of the passage, her primary purpose is revealed when she states, "But people who try to sell you this narrative are wrong."

(C) is incorrect. The author makes no comment on the outcome of the Civil War.

(D) is incorrect. The author asserts that, despite the popular identity narrative, the cause of the Civil War was actually very clear: "The Civil War was not a battle of cultural identities—it was a battle about slavery."

25. (A) is incorrect. The passage states that "vision does not become the dominant sense until around the age of 12 months."

(B) is correct. The passage states that "infants rely primarily on hearing."

(C) is incorrect. The sense of touch in not mentioned in the passage.

(D) is incorrect. The sense of smell is not mentioned in the passage.

MECHANICAL COMPREHENSION

1. **(B) is correct.** Moving the block farther from the brick changes the location of the fulcrum. The weight of the brick will have more torque since it is farther from the fulcrum; therefore it is going to take more force to lift. The increase in distance also will lift the board higher than before.

2. **(A) is correct.** Levers with a fulcrum that is between the effort and the resistance are always first-class levers.

3. **(A) is correct.** Adjacent gears rotate in the opposite directions. Gears 2 and 4 will move in the same direction, and Gears 1 and 3 will both move in the direction that is opposite to Gears 2 and 4.

4. **(B) is correct.** The larger the radius of a pulley, the slower it will turn. Because Pulley C has the largest radius, it will turn the slowest.

5. **(B) is correct.** The board is balanced when the net torque is zero, meaning the torque from each block is equal.

    $$T_1 = T_2$$
    $$F_1 l_1 = F_2 l_2$$
    $$40(3) = 60 l_2$$
    $$l_2 = \frac{120}{60} = \textbf{2 ft.}$$

6. **(C) is correct.** The figure shows a ramp acting as an inclined plane.

7. **(C) is correct.** The blocks will be at rest when the net force on the system is zero, meaning the total weight on the left side of the pulley must be equal to the weight on the right side. Block C needs to be 50 pounds so that there are 70 pounds on both sides of the pulley.

8. **(C) is correct.** When the bullet moves right and collides with the block, it will move the block the same direction. Since the block is attached to the string, it will also swing up.

9. **(A) is correct.** The weight of the air in the ball is much less than the same volume of water that was displaced. Therefore, the buoyant upward force is very large.

10. **(B) is correct.** The theoretical mechanical advantage is the total number of ropes that are in contact with the load, so the advantage is 2.

11. **(A) is correct.** The mass of an object is constant. The weight of an object depends on the force of gravity that the object experiences. The gravity of the moon is less than Earth's, so Object B will have the same mass but a smaller weight.

12. **(A) is correct.** The weight is evenly distributed on both sides of the object. Because B and C are helping each other carry the weight on the right side, A is bearing the most weight.

13. **(C) is correct.** To make air flow in the desired direction, open a valve on the opposite path. This causes a difference in pressure that will keep the air flowing on the desired path. To make the air flow through the top path, open all the valves on the bottom: 5, 6, and 7.

14. **(B) is correct.** Heat will transfer from the steel ball to the liquid. The equilibrium temperature depends on the masses of the objects and the specific heat of each object. Without knowing these values, the only guarantee is that the temperatures of the objects will be somewhere between 120°C and 150°C.

15. **(A) is correct.** The velocity of a fluid through a pipe is inversely related to the size of the pipe, so the water's velocity will go down when the diameter of the pipe goes up.

16. **(B) is correct.** Water flows into the tower at a rate of 140 gallons per hour and out at a rate of 3 gallons per minute, or 180 gallons per hour. The tower is losing 180 − 140 = 40 gallons of water per hour.

17. **(A) is correct.** The weight is closer to Scale A than it is to Scale B, so Scale A will have a higher reading. The fulcrum in this case is the center of the rod, so there is more weight on the left side of the fulcrum.

18. **(A) is correct.** The gas that is compressed into the smallest space will have the greatest pressure. Container A has the smallest volume, so it has the greatest pressure.

19. **(C) is correct.** The two charges are the same type, negative, and will therefore repel and move farther apart.

20. **(C) is correct.** Plug in the values for the resistors to get the equivalent resistance.

$$R_{eq} = R_1 + R_2 + ... + R_n$$
$$R_{eq} = 1 \text{ k}\Omega + 2 \text{ k}\Omega + 0.5 \text{ k}\Omega = 3.5 \text{ k}\Omega$$

21. **(A) is correct.** A conductor has free electrons that easily move current, while an insulator has restricted electrons that do not allow current to flow.

(B) is incorrect. Electrons are not created or destroyed by electronics materials. (They can be created or destroyed in nuclear reactions, like in the sun.)

(C) is incorrect. All materials will have heat created when electricity flows through them.

22. **(B) is correct.** A scale gives the weight of an object, not its mass. The scale reading is the same as the normal force that the object experiences. The object is moving upward, so the normal force has to be greater than the downward force of the weight. Thus, the scale will read a weight that is greater than 80 pounds.

23. **(B) is correct.** The net force on the object will be zero, so the mass is in equilibrium and will not accelerate.

24. **(A) is correct.** The height of the water moves up relative to the volume the object displaces, so the object with the higher volume will raise the water level higher. Density is the ratio of mass to volume, so if Objects A and B have the same mass, Object B must have a larger volume and thus a lower density.

25. **(A) is correct.** The current in the river will carry the boat downstream.

PRACTICE TEST TWO

MATH SKILLS

40 minutes

This section measures your knowledge of mathematical terms and principles. Each question is followed by four possible answers. You are to decide which one of the four choices is correct.

1. Simplify: $10^2 - 7(3 - 4) - 25$

(A) -12

(B) 2

(C) 68

(D) 82

2. Simplify: $17.38 - 19.26 + 14.2$

(A) 12.08

(B) 12.32

(C) 16.08

(D) 16.22

3. If a student answers 42 out of 48 questions correctly on a quiz, what percentage of questions did she answer correctly?

(A) 82.5%

(B) 85%

(C) 87.5%

(D) 90%

4. What is the remainder when 397 is divided by 4?

(A) 0

(B) 1

(C) 2

(D) 4

5. A teacher has 50 notebooks to hand out to students. If she has 16 students in her class, and each student receives 2 notebooks, how many notebooks will she have left over?

(A) 2

(B) 16

(C) 18

(D) 32

6. $3x^3 + 4x - (2x + 5y) + y =$

(A) $11x - 4y$

(B) $29x - 4y$

(C) $3x^3 + 2x - 4y$

(D) $3x^3 + 2x + y$

7. Allison used $2\frac{1}{2}$ cups of flour to make a cake, and $\frac{3}{4}$ of a cup of flour to make a pie. If she started with 4 cups of flour, how many cups of flour does she have left?

(A) $\frac{3}{4}$

(B) 1

(C) $\frac{5}{2}$

(D) $\frac{13}{4}$

8. Students board a bus at 7:45 a.m. and arrive at school at 8:20 a.m. How long are the students on the bus?

(A) 30 minutes

(B) 35 minutes

(C) 45 minutes

(D) 60 minutes

9. What is the area of the figure below?

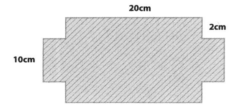

(A) 142 cm²

(B) 200 cm²

(C) 296 cm²

(D) 320 cm²

10. An ice chest contains 24 sodas, some regular and some diet. The ratio of diet soda to regular soda is 1:3. How many regular sodas are there in the ice chest?

(A) 1

(B) 4

(C) 18

(D) 24

11. Which expression is equivalent to dividing 300 by 12?

(A) $2(150 - 6)$

(B) $(300 \div 4) \div 6$

(C) $(120 \div 6) + (180 \div 6)$

(D) $(120 \div 12) + (180 \div 12)$

12. Out of 1560 students at Ward Middle School, 15% want to take French. Which expression represents how many students want to take French?

(A) $1560 \div 15$

(B) 1560×15

(C) 1560×0.15

(D) $1560 \div 0.15$

13. Which of the following is a solution of the given equation?
$4(m + 4)^2 - 4m^2 + 20 = 276$

(A) 3

(B) 6

(C) 12

(D) 24

14. At the grocery store, apples cost $1.89 per pound and oranges cost $2.19 per pound. How much would it cost to purchase 2 pounds of apples and 1.5 pounds of oranges?

(A) $6.62

(B) $7.07

(C) $7.14

(D) $7.22

15. Kendrick has $2,386.52 in his checking account. If he pays $792.00 for rent, $84.63 for groceries, and $112.15 for his car insurance, how much money will he have left in his account?

(A) $1,397.74

(B) $1,482.37

(C) $1,509.89

(D) $2,189.22

16. If a car uses 8 gallons of gas to travel 650 miles, how many miles can it travel using 12 gallons of gas?

(A) 870 miles

(B) 895 miles

(C) 915 miles

(D) 975 miles

17. A group of 20 friends is planning a road trip. They have 3 cars that seat 4 people, 3 cars that seat 5 people, and 1 car that seats 6 people. What is the fewest number of cars they can take on the trip if each person needs his or her own seat?

(A) 3 cars

(B) 4 cars

(C) 5 cars

(D) 6 cars

18. What is the percent increase in an employee's salary if it is raised from $57,000 to $60,000?

(A) 0.3%

(B) 3%

(C) 4%

(D) 5%

19. The formula for distance is $d = v \times t$, where v is the object's velocity and t is the time. How long will it take a plane to fly 4000 miles from Chicago to London if the plane flies at a constant rate of 500 mph?

(A) 3.5 hours

(B) 8 hours

(C) 20 hours

(D) 45 hours

20. 15 is 8% of what number?

(A) 1.2

(B) 53.3

(C) 120

(D) 187.5

21. A woman's dinner bill is $48.30. If she adds a 20% tip, what will she pay in total?

(A) $9.66

(B) $38.64

(C) $57.96

(D) $68.30

22. What is the surface area of a box that is 12 inches long, 18 inches wide, and 6 inches high?

(A) 144 in^2

(B) 396 in^2

(C) 412 in^2

(D) 792 in^2

23. There are 380 female students in a class. Male students make up 60% of the class. What is the total number of students in the class?

(A) 570

(B) 633

(C) 950

(D) 2,280

24. $(5 + \sqrt{5})(5 - \sqrt{5}) =$

(A) $10\sqrt{5}$

(B) 20

(C) 25

(D) $25\sqrt{5}$

25. $100x^2 + 25x =$

(A) $25(4x + x)$

(B) $25(4x^2 + x)$

(C) $25x(4x + 1)$

(D) $100x(x + 25x)$

READING COMPREHENSION

30 minutes

This section measures your ability to read and understand written material. Passages are followed by a series of multiple-choice questions. You are to choose the option that best answers the question based on the passage. No additional information or specific knowledge is needed.

Between November 15 and December 21, 1864, Major General William Tecumseh Sherman marched Union troops from the recently captured city of Atlanta to the port of Savannah. The goal was not only to capture the port city and secure Georgia for the Union, but also to destroy the Confederacy's infrastructure and demoralize its people. Sherman and his troops destroyed rail lines and burned buildings and fields. They packed only twenty days' worth of rations, foraging for the rest of their supplies from farms along the way. By the time they reached Savannah, they had destroyed 300 miles of railroad, countless cotton gins and mills, seized 4,000 mules, 13,000 head of cattle, 9.5 million pounds of corn, and 10.5 million pounds of fodder. Sherman estimated his troops inflicted $100 million in damages.

1. It can be inferred from the passage that the Confederacy
   (A) strongly resisted the actions of Sherman's troops.
   (B) was greatly weakened by the destruction.
   (C) used Sherman's March as a rallying point.
   (D) was relatively unaffected by the march.

The Gatling gun, a forerunner of the modern machine gun, was an early rapid-fire spring loaded, hand-cranked weapon. In 1861, Dr. Richard J. Gatling designed the gun to allow one person to fire many shots quickly. His goal was to reduce the death toll of war by decreasing the number of soldiers needed to fight. The gun consisted of a central shaft surrounded by six rotating barrels. A soldier turned a crank which rotated the shaft. As each barrel reached a particular point in the cycle, it fired, ejected its spent cartridge and loaded another. During this process, it cooled down, preparing it to fire again. The Gatling gun was first used in combat by the Union Army during the Civil War. However, each gun was purchased directly by individual commanders. The US Army did not purchase a Gatling gun until 1866.

2. The primary purpose of the passage is to
   (A) explain why the Gatling gun was harmful to troops.
   (B) critique the US Army's use of the Gatling gun.
   (C) describe the design and early history of the Gatling gun.
   (D) analyze the success of Dr. Gatling in achieving his goals.

American Cowslip: This plant grows spontaneously in Virginia and other parts of North America. It flowers in the beginning of May, and the seeds ripen in July, soon after which the stalks and leaves decay, so that the roots remain inactive till the following spring. It is propagated by offsets, which the roots put out freely when they are in a loose moist soil and a shady situation; the best time to remove the roots, and take away the offsets, is in August, after the leaves and stalks are decayed, that they may be fixed well in their new situation before the frost comes on.

William Curtis, *The Botanical Magazine*, 1790

3. According to the passage, which of the following is the best time to remove the roots of American Cowslip?

(A) August

(B) May

(C) July

(D) December

4. Which of the following is the meaning of *propagated* as used in the sentence?

(A) killed

(B) multiplied

(C) extracted

(D) concealed

In December of 1945, Germany launched its last major offensive campaign of World War II, pushing through the dense forests of the Ardennes region of Belgium, France, and Luxembourg. The attack, designed to block the Allies from the Belgian port of Antwerp and to split their lines, caught the Allied forces by surprise. Due to troop positioning, the Americans bore the brunt of the attack, incurring 100,000 deaths, the highest number of casualties of any battle during the war. However, after a month of grueling fighting in the bitter cold, a lack of fuel and a masterful American military strategy resulted in an Allied victory that sealed Germany's fate.

5. In the last sentence, the word *grueling* most nearly means

(A) exhausting

(B) costly

(C) intermittent

(D) ineffective

For thirteen years, a spacecraft called *Cassini* has been on an exploratory mission to Saturn. The spacecraft was designed not to return but to end its journey by diving into Saturn's atmosphere. This dramatic ending will provide scientists with unprecedented information about Saturn's atmosphere and its magnetic and gravitational fields. First, however, *Cassini* will pass Saturn's largest moon, Titan, where it will record any changes in Titan's curious methane lakes, gathering information about potential seasons on the planet-sized moon. Then it will pass through the unexplored region between Saturn itself and its famous rings. Scientists hope to learn how old the rings are and to directly examine the particles that make them up. It is likely that the spectacular end to *Cassini* will introduce new questions for future exploration.

6. According to the passage, scientists want to learn more about Titan's

(A) gravity, based on examination of its magnetic field.

(B) rings, based on the particles that compose them.

(C) seasons, based on changes to its lakes.

(D) age, based on analysis of its minerals and gases.

Researchers at the University of California, Berkeley, decided to tackle an age-old problem: why shoelaces come untied. They recorded the shoelaces of a volunteer walking on a treadmill by attaching devices to record the acceleration, or g-force, experienced by the knot. The results were surprising. A shoelace knot experiences more g-force from a person walking than any rollercoaster can generate. However, if the person simply stomped or swung their feet—the two movements that make up a walker's stride—the g-force was not enough to undo the knots. Researchers also found that while the knot loosened slowly at first, once it reached a certain laxness, it simply fell apart.

7. The author includes a comparison to rollercoasters in order to
   (A) illustrate the intensity of force experienced by the knots.
   (B) describe an experiment undertaken by researchers.
   (C) critique a main finding of the experiment.
   (D) provide further evidence to support the study's conclusion.

Skin coloration and markings have an important role to play in the world of snakes. Those intricate diamonds, stripes, and swirls help the animals hide from predators, but perhaps most importantly (for us humans, anyway), the markings can also indicate whether the snake is venomous. While it might seem counterintuitive for a venomous snake to stand out in bright red or blue, that fancy costume tells any nearby predator that approaching him would be a bad idea.

If you see a flashy-looking snake in the woods, though, those markings don't necessarily mean it's venomous: some snakes have found a way to ward off predators without the actual venom. The scarlet kingsnake, for example, has very similar markings to the venomous coral snake with whom it frequently shares a habitat. However, the kingsnake is actually nonvenomous; it's merely pretending to be dangerous to eat. A predatory hawk or eagle, usually hunting from high in the sky, can't tell the difference between the two species, and so the kingsnake gets passed over and lives another day.

8. What is the author's primary purpose in writing this essay?
   (A) To explain how the markings on a snake are related to whether it's venomous.
   (B) To teach readers the difference between coral snakes and kingsnakes.
   (C) To illustrate why snakes are dangerous.
   (D) To demonstrate how animals survive in difficult environments.

9. What can the reader conclude from the passage above?
   (A) The kingsnake is dangerous to humans.
   (B) The coral snake and the kingsnake are both hunted by the same predators.
   (C) It's safe to handle snakes in the woods because you can easily tell whether they're poisonous.
   (D) The kingsnake changes its markings when hawks or eagles are close by.

10. Which statement is NOT a detail from the passage?
    (A) Predators will avoid eating kingsnakes because their markings are similar to those on coral snakes.
    (B) Kingsnakes and coral snakes live in the same habitats.
    (C) The coral snake uses its coloration to hide from predators.
    (D) The kingsnake is not venomous.

11. What is the meaning of the word *intricate* in the first paragraph?

    (A) complex

    (B) colorful

    (C) purposeful

    (D) changeable

At midnight on Saturday, August 12, 1961, units of the East German army moved into position and began closing the border between East and West Berlin. Destroying streets that ran parallel to the border to make them impassable, they installed ninety-seven miles of barbed wire and fences around West Berlin and another twenty-seven miles along the border between West and East Berlin. By Sunday morning the border was completely shut down. Families woke up that morning suddenly divided, and some East Berliners with jobs in the west were unable to get to work. West Berlin was now an isolated island surrounded by a communist government hostile to its existence.

12. The primary purpose of the passage is to

    (A) describe the impact of the closing of the Berlin border.

    (B) analyze East Germany's motives for closing the Berlin border.

    (C) explain the Western response to the closing of the Berlin border.

    (D) inform the reader about the methods used to close the Berlin border.

In 1989, almost a million Chinese university students descended on central Beijing, protesting for increased democracy and calling for the resignation of Communist Party leaders. For three weeks, they marched, chanted, and held daily vigils in the city's Tiananmen Square. The protests had widespread support in China, particularly among factory workers who cheered them on. For Westerners watching, it seemed to be the beginning of a political revolution in China, so the world was stunned when, on July 4, Chinese troops and security police stormed the square, firing into the crowd. Chaos erupted with some students trying to fight back by throwing stones and setting fire to military vehicles. Tens of thousands more attempted to flee. While official numbers were never given, observers estimated anywhere from 300 to thousands of people were killed, while 10,000 were arrested.

13. It can be inferred from the passage that after July 4

    (A) the protest movement in China gained increasing support.

    (B) Western countries intervened on behalf of the university protestors.

    (C) factory workers took action in defense of the protestors.

    (D) the movement for increased democracy in China fell apart.

The Scream of Nature by Edvard Munch is one of the world's best known and most desirable artworks. While most people think of it as a single painting, the iconic creation actually has four different versions: two paintings and two pastels. In 2012, one of the pastels earned the fourth highest price paid for a painting at auction when it was sold for almost $120 million. The three others are not for sale; the Munch Museum in Oslo holds a painted version and a pastel version, while the National Gallery in Oslo holds the other painting. However, the desire to acquire them has been just as strong: in 1994 the National Gallery's version was stolen, and in 2004 the painting at the Munch Museum was stolen at gunpoint in the middle of the day. Both paintings were eventually recovered.

14. The primary purpose of the passage is to

(A) describe the image depicted in *The Scream in Nature*.

(B) explain the origin of the painting *The Scream in Nature*.

(C) clarify the number of versions of *The Scream in Nature* that exist.

(D) prove the high value of *The Scream in Nature*.

After World War I, powerful political and social forces pushed for a return to normalcy in the United States. The result was disengagement from the larger world and increased focus on American economic growth and personal enjoyment. Caught in the middle of this was a cache of American writers, raised on the values of the prewar world and frustrated with what they viewed as the superficiality and materialism of postwar American culture. Many of them, like Ernest Hemingway and F. Scott Fitzgerald, fled to Paris, where they became known as the "lost generation," creating a trove of literary works criticizing their home culture and delving into their own feelings of alienation.

15. In the third sentence, the word *cache* most nearly means

(A) a group of the same type.

(B) a majority segment.

(C) an organization.

(D) a dispersed number.

Increasingly, companies are turning to subcontracting services rather than hiring full-time employees. This provides companies with many advantages like greater flexibility, reduced legal responsibility to employees, and lower possibility of unionization within the company. However, it has also led to increasing confusion and uncertainty over the legal definition of employment. Recently, the courts have grappled with questions about the hiring company's responsibility in maintaining fair labor practices. Companies argue that they delegate that authority to the subcontractors, while unions and other worker advocate groups argue that companies still have a legal obligation to the workers who contribute to their business.

16. The primary purpose of the passage is to

(A) critique the labor practices of modern companies.

(B) explain why companies prefer subcontracting work.

(C) highlight a debate within the business and labor community.

(D) describe a recent court decision related to labor practices.

In a remote nature preserve in northeastern Siberia, scientists are attempting to recreate the subarctic steppe grassland ecosystem that flourished there during the last Ice Age. The area today is dominated by forests, but the lead scientists of the project believe the forested terrain was neither a natural development nor environmentally advantageous. They believe that if they can restore the grassland, they will be able to slow climate change by slowing the thawing of the permafrost which lies beneath the tundra. Key to this undertaking is restoring the wildlife to the region, including wild horses, musk oxen, bison, and yak. Most ambitiously, the scientists hope to revive the wooly mammoth species which was key in trampling the ground and knocking down the trees, helping to keep the land free for grasses to grow.

17. In the fourth sentence, the word *advantageous* most nearly means

(A) beneficial

(B) damaging

(C) useful

(D) appropriate

It has now been two decades since the introduction of thermonuclear fusion weapons into the military inventories of the great powers, and more than a decade since the United States, Great Britain, and the Soviet Union ceased to test nuclear weapons in the atmosphere. Today our understanding of the technology of thermonuclear weapons seems highly advanced, but our knowledge of the physical and biological consequences of nuclear war is continuously evolving.

United States Arms Control and Disarmament Agency,
Worldwide Effects of Nuclear War: Some Perspectives, 1998

18. A student has written the paragraph below as an introduction to a paper. Which of the following is most likely the topic of the paper?

(A) the impact of thermonuclear weapons on the military

(B) the technology of thermonuclear weapons

(C) atmospheric testing of nuclear weapons

(D) the physical and biological consequences of nuclear war

In recent decades, jazz has been associated with New Orleans and festivals like Mardi Gras, but in the 1920s, jazz was a booming trend whose influence reached into many aspects of American culture. In fact, the years between World War I and the Great Depression were known as the Jazz Age, a term coined by F. Scott Fitzgerald in his famous novel The Great Gatsby. Sometimes also called the Roaring Twenties, this time period saw major urban centers experiencing new economic, cultural, and artistic vitality. In the United States, musicians flocked to cities like New York and Chicago, which would become famous hubs for jazz musicians. Ella Fitzgerald, for example, moved from Virginia to New York City to begin her much-lauded singing career, and jazz pioneer Louis Armstrong got his big break in Chicago.

Jazz music was played by and for a more expressive and freed populace than the United States had previously seen. Women gained the right to vote and were openly seen drinking and dancing to jazz music. This period marked the emergence of the flapper, a woman determined to make a statement about her new role in society. Jazz music also provided the soundtrack for the explosion of African American art and culture now known as the Harlem Renaissance. In addition to Fitzgerald and Armstrong, numerous musicians, including Duke Ellington, Fats Waller, and Bessie Smith, promoted their distinctive and complex music as an integral part of the emerging African American culture.

19. What is the main idea of the passage?

(A) People should associate jazz music with the 1920s, not modern New Orleans.

(B) Jazz music played an important role in many cultural movements of the 1920s.

(C) Many famous jazz musicians began their careers in New York City and Chicago.

(D) African Americans were instrumental in launching jazz into mainstream culture.

20. What is the author's primary purpose in writing this essay?

(A) to explain the role jazz musicians played in the Harlem Renaissance

(B) to inform the reader about the many important musicians playing jazz in the 1920s

(C) to discuss how jazz influenced important cultural movements in the 1920s

(D) to provide a history of jazz music in the 20th century

21. Which of the following is NOT a fact stated in the passage?

A) The years between World War I and the Great Depression were known as the Jazz Age.

B) Ella Fitzgerald and Louis Armstrong both moved to New York City to start their music careers.

C) Women danced to jazz music during the 1920s to make a statement about their role in society.

D) Jazz music was an integral part of the emerging African American culture of the 1920s.

22. What can the reader conclude from the passage above?

(A) F. Scott Fitzgerald supported jazz musicians in New York and Chicago.

(B) Jazz music is no longer as popular as it once was.

(C) Both women and African Americans used jazz music as a way of expressing their newfound freedom.

(D) Flappers and African American musicians worked together to produce jazz music.

Alfie closed his eyes and took several deep breaths. He was trying to ignore the sounds of the crowd, but even he had to admit that it was hard not to notice the tension in the stadium. He could feel 50,000 sets of eyes burning through his skin—this crowd expected perfection from him. He took another breath and opened his eyes, setting his sights on the soccer ball resting peacefully in the grass. One shot, just one last shot, between his team and the championship. He didn't look up at the goalie, who was jumping nervously on the goal line just a few yards away. Afterward, he would swear he didn't remember anything between the referee's whistle and the thunderous roar of the crowd.

23. Which of the following conclusions is best supported by the passage?

(A) Alfie passed out on the field and was unable to take the shot.

(B) The goalie blocked Alfie's shot.

(C) Alfie scored the goal and won his team the championship.

(D) The referee declared the game a tie.

In its most basic form, geography is the study of space; more specifically, it studies the physical space of the earth and the ways in which it interacts with, shapes, and is shaped by its habitants. Geographers look at the world from a spatial perspective. This means that at the center of all geographic study is the question, *where?* For geographers, the *where* of any interaction, event, or development is a crucial element to understanding it.

This question of *where* can be asked in a variety of fields of study, so there are many sub-disciplines of geography. These can be organized into four main categories: 1) regional studies, which examine the characteristics of a particular place; 2) topical studies, which look at a single physical or human feature that impacts the whole world; 3) physical studies, which focus on the physical features of Earth; and 4) human studies, which examine the relationship between human activity and the environment.

24. A researcher studying the relationship between farming and river systems would be engaged in which of the following geographical sub-disciplines?

   (A) regional studies

   (B) topical studies

   (C) physical studies

   (D) human studies

The study showed that private tutoring is providing a significant advantage to those students who are able to afford it. Researchers looked at the grades of students who had received free tutoring through the school versus those whose parents had paid for private tutors. The study included 2500 students in three high schools across four grade levels. The study found that private tutoring corresponded with a rise in grade point average (GPA) of 0.5 compared to students who used the school's free tutor service and 0.7 compared to students who used no tutoring. After reviewing the study, the board is recommending that the school restructure its free tutor service to provide a more equitable education for all students.

25. Which of the following would weaken the author's argument?

   (A) the fact that the cited study was funded by a company that provides discounted tutoring through schools

   (B) a study showing differences in standardized test scores between students at schools in different neighborhoods

   (C) a statement signed by local teachers stating that they do not provide preferential treatment in the classroom or when grading

   (D) a study showing that GPA does not strongly correlate with success in college

MECHANICAL COMPREHENSION

15 minutes

This section measures your understanding of basic mechanical principles. Each question is followed by three possible answers. You are to decide which one of the three choices is correct.

1.

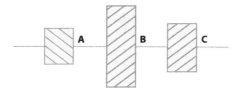

Gear C is intended to mesh with

(A) Gear A only.

(B) Gear B only.

(C) Gear E only.

2.

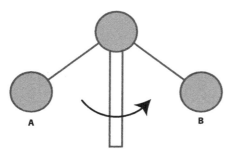

If the shaft shown in the figure above is spun in the opposite direction but maintains the same speed, balls A and B will

(A) move down.

(B) move up.

(C) stay at the same level.

3. A 140-pound woman jumps off a 700-pound stationary raft that is in a river and travels a distance of 10 feet to right. If the water in the river is at rest, the raft will move

(A) 2 feet to the right.

(B) 2 feet to the left.

(C) 4 feet to the left.

4.

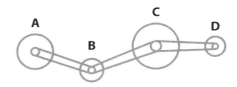

If Pulley B is the driver and turns clockwise, which pulley turns the slowest?

(A) Pulley A turns the slowest.

(B) Pulley C turns the slowest.

(C) Pulley D turns the slowest.

5. A brake pedal with the load between the fulcrum and the effort is an example of a

(A) first-class lever.

(B) second-class lever.

(C) third-class lever.

6.

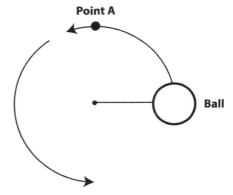

A ball attached to a string is being twirled in a circle. If the string is cut at point A, in what direction will the ball move?

(A) The ball will move left.

(B) The ball will move right.

(C) The ball will continue moving in a circle.

7.

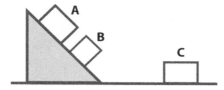

Blocks A, B, and C are identical. If the same force is applied to Blocks A, B, and C, which of the following will be true?

(A) The acceleration of A is greater than B, which is greater than C.

(B) The acceleration of A is the same as B, which is greater than C.

(C) The acceleration of B is greater than A but less than C.

8. [Fig 21]

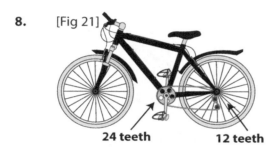

24 teeth   **12 teeth**

On the bicycle shown in the figure, there are 12 teeth on the rear sprocket and 24 teeth on the front sprocket. Each time the rear wheel goes around twice, the pedals go around

(A) 1 time.

(B) 2 times.

(C) 3 times.

9. A wooden ball and a steel ball are both held at 15°C. Which ball will feel colder and why?

(A) The wooden ball will feel colder because it has greater conductivity.

(B) The steel ball will feel colder because it has greater conductivity.

(C) The objects will feel the same because they have the same temperature.

10.

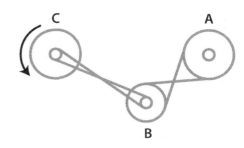

Pulley B will rotate

(A) in the same direction as Pulley A but opposite of Pulley C.

(B) in the same direction as both Pulley A and Pulley C.

(C) in the opposite direction of both Pulley A and Pulley C.

11.

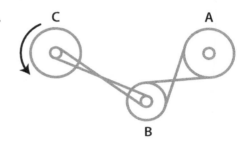

Pulley A will rotate

(A) faster than both Pulley B and Pulley C.

(B) slower than both Pulley B and Pulley C.

(C) slower than Pulley B but with the same speed as Pulley C.

12.

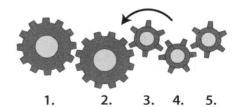

1.   2.   3.   4.   5.

Which of the gears are moving in the opposite direction of Gear 3?

(A) Gear 1 and Gear 4 only

(B) Gear 2 and Gear 4 only

(C) Gear 2 and Gear 5 only

13.

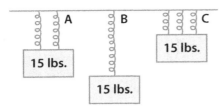

Three 15-pound blocks are attached to the ceiling using identical springs, as shown. If A, B, and C are the forces on their respective springs, which of the following is true?

(A) B is greater than C but less than A.

(B) C is greater than A but less than B.

(C) A is greater than C but less than B.

14.

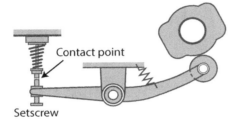

As Cam 1 makes two complete turns, how many times does the set screw hit the contact point?

(A) 2

(B) 4

(C) 5

15.

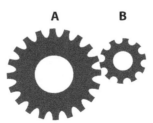

If Gear A makes 15 revolutions, Gear B will make

(A) 30 revolutions.

(B) 25 revolutions.

(C) 22 revolutions.

16.

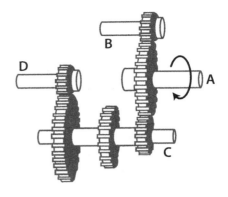

Which shafts are turning in the same direction as Shaft A?

(A) Shafts D and E only

(B) Shafts B and D only

(C) Shafts B and C only

17.

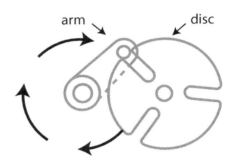

The figure shows a slotted disc turned by a pin on a rotating arm. Three revolutions of the arm turns the disc

(A) $\frac{1}{3}$ turn.

(B) 1 turn.

(C) 3 turns.

18.

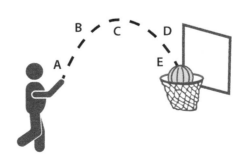

At which of the points shown above is the basketball moving the fastest?

(A) D only

(B) A and E

(C) B and C

19. Two negative charges are held at a distance of 1 m from each other. When the charges are released, they will

   (A) remain at rest.

   (B) move closer together.

   (C) move farther apart.

Use the figure below for questions 20 and 21.

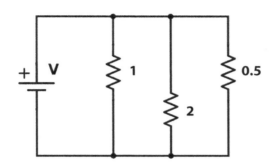

20. Find the equivalent resistance, R_{eq}, for the circuit in the figure above.

   (A) 0.3 kΩ

   (B) 0.5 kΩ

   (C) 3.5 kΩ

21. What is the voltage across a 1 kΩ resistor if 1 mA is flowing through it?

   (A) 0.1 V

   (B) 1 V

   (C) 10 V

22. Which of these objects would be the hardest for an astronaut to move in outer space?

   (A) a wrench

   (B) another astronaut

   (C) the International Space Station

23. A single pulley is attached to the ceiling. It is holding a rope that is attached to the floor on one side and a person of weight 100 N on the other. What is the tension in the rope?

   (A) 0 N

   (B) 50 N

   (C) 100 N

24.

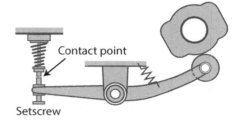

As Cam 1 makes two complete turns, how many times does the set screw hit the contact point?

   (A) 2

   (B) 4

   (C) 5

25.

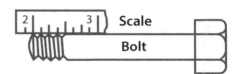

The number of threads per inch for the bolt shown in the figure is

   (A) 2.

   (B) 4.

   (C) 8.

ANSWER KEY

MATH SKILLS

1. **(D)**

    Simplify using PEMDAS.

    $10^2 - 7(3 - 4) - 25$

    $= 10^2 - 7(-1) - 25$

    $= 100 + 7 - 25$

    $= 107 - 25 = \mathbf{82}$

2. **(B)**

    Align the decimals and add/subtract from left to right.

    $17.38 - 19.26 + 14.2$

    $= (-1.88) + 14.2 = \mathbf{12.32}$

3. **(C)**

    Use the formula for percentages.

    $percent = \frac{part}{whole}$

    $= \frac{42}{48}$

    $= 0.875 = \mathbf{87.5\%}$

4. **(B)**

    Find the highest possible multiple of 4 that is less than or equal to 397, and then subtract to find the remainder.

    $99 \times 4 = 396$

    $397 - 396 = \mathbf{1}$

5. **(C)**

    If each student receives 2 notebooks, the teacher will need $16 \times 2 = 32$ notebooks. After handing out the notebooks, she will have $50 - 32 = 18$ notebooks left.

6. **(C)**

    Apply the distributive property, and then combine like terms.

    $3x^3 + 4x - (2x + 5y) + y$

    $= 3x^3 + 4x - 2x - 5y + y$

    $= \mathbf{3x^3 + 2x - 4y}$

7. **(A)**

    Add the fractions and subtract the result from the amount of flour Allison started with

    $2\frac{1}{2} + \frac{3}{4} = \frac{5}{2} + \frac{3}{4} = \frac{10}{4} + \frac{3}{4} = \frac{13}{4}$

    $4 - \frac{13}{4} = \frac{16}{4} - \frac{13}{4} = \mathbf{\frac{3}{4}}$

8. **(B)**

    There are 15 minutes between 7:45 a.m. and 8:00 a.m. and 20 minutes between 8:00 a.m. and 8:20 a.m.

    15 minutes + 20 minutes = **35 minutes**

9. (D)

Find the area of the complete rectangle and subtract the area of the missing corners.

rectangle: $A = lw = (20 + 2 + 2) \times (10 + 2 + 2) = 336$ cm²

corners: $A = 4(lw) = 4(2 \times 2) = 16$ cm²

$336 - 16 = \textbf{320 cm}^2$

10. (C)

One way to find the answer is to draw a picture.

Put 24 cans into groups of 4. One out of every 4 cans is diet (light gray) so there is 1 light gray can for every 3 dark gray cans. That leaves 18 dark gray cans (regular soda).

Alternatively, solve the problem using ratios.

$\frac{Regular}{Total} = \frac{3}{4} = \frac{x}{24}$

$4x = 72$

$\textbf{\textit{x} = 18}$

11. (D)

$300 \div 12 = 25$

Test each answer choice to see if it equals 25.

A. $2(150 - 6)$

$= 2(144)$

$= 288 \neq 25$

B. $(300 \div 4) \div 6$

$= 75 \div 6$

$= 12.5 \neq 25$

C. $(120 \div 6) + (180 \div 6)$

$= 20 + 30$

$= 50 \neq 25$

D. $(120 \div 12) + (180 \div 12)$

$= (10) + (15)$

$= \textbf{25}$

12. (C)

Use the formula for finding percentages. Express the percentage as a decimal.

part = whole × percentage = **1560 × 0.15**

13. (B)

Plug each value into the equation.

$4(3 + 4)^2 - 4(3)^2 + 20 = 180 \neq 276$

$4(6 + 4)^2 - 4(6)^2 + 20 = \textbf{276}$

$4(12 + 4)^2 - 4(12)^2 + 20 = 468 \neq 276$

$4(24 + 4)^2 - 4(24)^2 + 20 = 852 \neq 276$

14. (B)

Multiply the cost per pounds by the number of pounds purchased to find the cost of each fruit.

apples: $2(1.89) = 3.78$

oranges: $1.5(2.19) = 3.285$

$3.78 + 3.285 = 7.065 = \textbf{\$7.07}$

15. (A)

Subtract the amount of the bills from the amount in the checking account.

$792.00 + 84.63 + 112.15 = 988.78$

$2,386.52 - 988.78 = \textbf{\$1,397.74}$

16. (D)

Set up a proportion and solve.

$\frac{8}{650} = \frac{12}{x}$

$12(650) = 8x$

$\textbf{\textit{x} = 975 miles}$

17. (B)

Add together the seats in the cars until there are 20.

$6 + 5 = 11$

$6 + 5 + 5 = 16$

$6 + 5 + 5 + 5 = 21$

They fewest number of cars that will seat 20 people is **4 cars**.

18. (D)

Use the formula for percent increase.

percent increase $= \dfrac{amount\ of\ change}{original\ amount}$

$= \dfrac{3,000}{60,000} = 0.05 = \textbf{5\%}$

19. (B)

Plug the given values into the equation and solve for t.

$d = v \times t$

$4000 = 500 \times t$

$t = \textbf{8 hours}$

20. (D)

Create a proportion and solve.

$\dfrac{\text{part}}{\text{whole}} = \dfrac{\%}{100}$

$\dfrac{15}{x} = \dfrac{8}{100}$

$15(100) = 8(x)$

$x = \textbf{187.5}$

21. (C)

Multiply the total bill by 0.2 (20%) to find the amount of the tip. Then add the tip to the total.

$\$48.30 \times 0.2 = \$9.66$

$\$48.30 + \$9.66 = \textbf{\$57.96}$

22. (D)

Use the formula for the surface area of a rectangular prism.

$SA = 2lw + 2lh + 2wh$

$SA = 2(12)(18) + 2(12)(6) + 2(18)(6)$

$= 432 + 216 + 144 = \textbf{792 in}^2$

23. (C)

If 60% of the students are male, then 40% of the students are female. Create a proportion and solve.

$\dfrac{\text{part}}{\text{whole}} = \dfrac{\%}{100}$

$\dfrac{380}{x} = \dfrac{40}{100}$

$380(100) = 40(x)$

$x = \textbf{950}$

24. (B)

Use the distributive property to multiply the binomial expressions.

$5(5 - \sqrt{5}) + \sqrt{5}(5 - \sqrt{5})$

$= 25 - 5\sqrt{5} + 5\sqrt{5} - 5$

$= \textbf{20}$

25. (C)

Factor out the greatest common factor.

$100x^2 + 25x = \textbf{25x(4x + 1)}$

READING COMPREHENSION

1. (A) is incorrect. The author does not provide enough detailed evidence to reasonably infer the Confederate reaction to the march.

    (B) is correct. The author describes the level of destruction in detail, suggesting it had a significant negative impact on the Confederacy.

    (C) is incorrect. Again, as in option A, the author does not describe any response to the march.

    (D) is incorrect. The author writes, "Sherman estimated his troops inflicted $100 million in damages."

2. (A) is incorrect. The author does not address the impact of the gun on troops.

    (B) is incorrect. The author does not offer an opinion on the use of the Gatling gun.

    (C) is correct. The author explains why the gun was created, how it functions, and how it was initially used.

    (D) is incorrect. The author does not describe the impact of Gatling gun on combat fatalities.

3. **(A) is correct.** The passage states that "the best time to remove the roots, and take away the offsets, is in August."

    (B) is incorrect. The passage states that the American Cowslip "flowers in the beginning of May."

    (C) is incorrect. The passage suggests that "the seeds [of the American Cowslip] ripen in July."

    (D) is incorrect. The author states that the time to remove the roots is in August "before the frost comes on."

4. (A) is incorrect. The author indicates that the American Cowslip "is propagated by offsets[,]" which

    should be removed and replanted in order allow the species to reproduce.

    (B) is correct. *Multiplied* best describes the passage's description of how the plant reproduces by producing offsets.

    (C) is incorrect. The author indicates that the American Cowslip "is propagated by offsets[,]" which should be removed and replanted in order allow the species to reproduce.

    (D) is incorrect. The author indicates that the American Cowslip "is propagated by offsets[,]" which should be removed and replanted in order allow the species to reproduce.

5. **(A) is correct.** The context implies that the fighting was intense and tiring.

    (B) is incorrect. Nothing in the passage addresses the price of the battle.

    (C) is incorrect. The passage indicates nothing about the pattern of fighting.

    (D) is incorrect. The author states that the fighting ultimately led to a US victory.

6. (A) is incorrect. The author discusses plans to study magnetic and gravitational fields on Saturn, not Titan.

    (B) is incorrect. The author writes, "Then it will pass through the unexplored region between Saturn itself and its famous rings." The passage does not mention any rings on Titan.

    (C) is correct. The author writes, "… it will record any changes in Titan's curious methane lakes, providing information about potential seasons on the planet-sized moon."

    (D) is incorrect. The author refers to the rings of Saturn, not to Titan, when stating, "Scientists hope to learn how old the rings are."

7. **(A) is correct.** The author writes, "a shoelace knot experiences greater g-force than any rollercoaster can generate," helping the reader understand the strength of the g-force experienced by the knots.

(B) is incorrect. The author does not describe any actual experiments involving rollercoasters.

(C) is incorrect. The author does not assess the findings of the experiment.

(D) is incorrect. The rollercoaster reference is a comparison, not specific evidence.

8. **(A) is correct.** The passage indicates that a snakes' "intricate diamonds, stripes, and swirls help the animals hide from predators, but perhaps most importantly (for us humans, anyway), the markings can also indicate whether the snake is venomous."

(B) is incorrect. Though the author does mention one difference between the kingsnake and the coral snake, this is not the primary purpose of the passage.

(C) is incorrect. The author does not indicate why snakes are dangerous, only that some of them are.

(D) is incorrect. Though the author does provide some examples of this, this answer choice is more general, while the passage focused on snakes in particular.

9. (A) is incorrect. The author mentions that "the kingsnake is actually nonvenomous" but provides no more information about whether the kingsnake poses a danger to humans.

(B) is correct. The final paragraph of the passage states that the two species "frequently [share] a habitat" and that "[a] predatory hawk or eagle, usually hunting from high in the sky, can't tell the difference between the two species, and so the kingsnake gets passed over and lives another day."

(C) is incorrect. The author does not imply that it is easy to tell the difference between venomous and nonvenomous snakes, only that it is possible.

(D) is incorrect. The final paragraph states that the kingsnake "has very similar marking to the venomous coral snake" and does not indicate that these markings change with circumstances.

10. (A) is incorrect. The second paragraph states that "[a] predatory hawk or eagle, usually hunting from high in the sky, can't tell the difference between the two species, and so the kingsnake gets passed over and lives another day."

(B) is incorrect. The second paragraph states that "[t]he scarlet kingsnake, for example, has very similar markings to the venomous coral snake with whom it frequently shares a habitat."

(C) is correct. The first paragraph states that "[w]hile it might seem counterintuitive for a venomous snake to stand out in bright red or blue, that fancy costume tells any nearby predator that approaching him would be a bad idea." The coral snake's markings do not allow it to hide from predators but rather to "ward [them] off[.]"

(D) is incorrect. The second paragraph states that "the kingsnake is actually nonvenomous; it's merely pretending to be dangerous to eat."

11. **(A) is correct.** The passage states that "intricate diamonds, stripes, and swirls help the animals hide from predators[,]" implying that these markings are complex enough to allow the animals to blend in with their surroundings.

(B) is incorrect. The passage indicates that colorful markings do not allow the animals to hide but rather to ward off predators, so the word *colorful* does not apply in the context of the sentence.

(C) is incorrect. This answer choice does not fit in the context of the sentence, as the animals do not choose their markings.

(D) is incorrect. The author does not suggest that animals' markings are changeable.

12. **(A) is correct.** The passage describes how the closing of the border affected the geography of the city and the lives of Berliners.

(B) is incorrect. The author does not explain why the border was closed.

(C) is incorrect. The author does not describe the response to the border closing.

(D) is incorrect. The author explains that the East German army closed off West Berlin using barbed wire and fences, but this is not the primary purpose of the passage.

13. (A) is incorrect. There is no evidence that the protest movement was successful; in fact, the passage implies the opposite.

(B) is incorrect. While the author states that Western countries observed the events in China, there is no evidence they became involved.

(C) is incorrect. There is no evidence in the passage that factory workers had any involvement beyond "cheering on" the protestors.

(D) is correct. The author writes, "it seemed to be the beginning of a political revolution in China, so the world was stunned when, on July 4, Chinese troops and security police stormed the square," stifling any possibility of democratic revolution.

14. (A) is incorrect. The passage does not describe the actual artwork at all.

(B) is incorrect. The author names the artist who made the painting but states nothing else about its origin.

(C) is incorrect. While the author does state that there are four versions of the artwork, this is not the primary purpose of the passage.

(D) is correct. The author writes, "*The Scream of Nature* by Edvard Munch is one of the world's best known and most desirable artworks."

15. **(A) is correct.** The author goes on to describe the shared perspectives of these writers.

(B) is incorrect. The author does not indicate the number of writers.

(C) is incorrect. The author provides no context that implies they were an organized group, simply that they shared certain traits.

(D) is incorrect. The author states that they gathered in one place—Paris.

16. (A) is incorrect. The author does not express an opinion on labor practices.

(B) is incorrect. While the author does explain the advantages of subcontracting for companies, this is not the primary purpose of the passage.

(C) is correct. The author presents the reasons for the debate and both sides of the argument.

(D) is incorrect. The author states that there have been related court cases but does not detail them.

17. **(A) is correct.** The author goes on to explain that the development of forests was not good for the environment: scientists believe grasslands would slow climate change.

(B) is incorrect. The author says that the forests are harmful to climate.

(C) is incorrect. The author explains that forests are harmful to the environment in this situation, and that grasslands would combat climate change. The word *useful* is too weak in this context.

(D) is incorrect. The word *appropriate* does not make sense in this context.

18. (A) is incorrect. The passage implies that "the physical and biological consequences of nuclear war" have

impacts that reach much further than the military.

(B) is incorrect. The second part of the second sentence suggests that the consequences of nuclear war—rather than the specific technology of nuclear weapons—are the focus of this student's paper.

(C) is incorrect. The author mentions the decision by world powers to cease testing nuclear weapons in the atmosphere; however, this is only one detail and is likely not the focus of the essay as a whole.

(D) is correct. The passage gives a short history of thermonuclear weapons and then introduces its main topic—the physical and biological consequences of nuclear war.

19. (A) is incorrect. While the author points out that jazz is often associated with New Orleans, he does not indicate that this is a problem or that people should change how they think about jazz.

(B) is correct. The author writes that "[j]azz music was played by and for a more expressive and freed populace than the United States had previously seen." In addition to "the emergence of the flapper[,]" the 1920s saw "the explosion of African American art and culture now known as the Harlem Renaissance."

(C) is incorrect. Though this is mentioned in the passage, it is not the main idea.

(D) is incorrect. Though this is stated at the end of the passage, it is not the main idea.

20. (A) is incorrect. The author writes, "Jazz music also provided the soundtrack for the explosion of African American art and culture now known as the Harlem Renaissance." However, this is not the primary purpose of the passage.

(B) is incorrect. Though the author names many of the important jazz musicians who were playing during the 1920s, this is not the primary purpose of the passage.

(C) is correct. The author opens the passage saying, "In recent decades, jazz has been associated with New Orleans and festivals like Mardi Gras, but in the 1920s, jazz was a booming trend whose influence reached into many aspects of American culture." He then goes on to elaborate on what these movements were.

(D) is incorrect. The author discusses the effects of jazz music on arts and culture in the 1920s but does not go into the history of the art.

21. (A) is incorrect. In the first paragraph, the author writes, "In fact, the years between World War I and the Great Depression were known as the Jazz Age, a term coined by F. Scott Fitzgerald in his famous novel *The Great Gatsby*."

(B) is correct. At the end of the first paragraph, the author writes, "Ella Fitzgerald, for example, moved from Virginia to New York City to begin her much-lauded singing career, and jazz pioneer Louis Armstrong got his big break in Chicago."

(C) is incorrect. At the beginning of the second paragraph, the author writes, "Women gained the right to vote and were openly seen drinking and dancing to jazz music. This period marked the emergence of the flapper, a woman determined to make a statement about her new role in society."

(D) is incorrect. Toward the end of the second paragraph, the author writes, "Jazz music also provided the soundtrack for the explosion of African American art and culture now known as the Harlem Renaissance."

22. (A) is incorrect. The author states that the term *Jazz Age* was "coined by F. Scott Fitzgerald in his famous novel *The Great Gatsby*" but does not

elaborate on Fitzgerald's relationship to the artists of the age.

(B) is incorrect. The author does not discuss the current popularity of jazz, only that it is often associated with New Orleans.

(C) is correct. The author writes that "[j]azz music was played by and for a more expressive and freed populace than the United States had previously seen." In addition to "the emergence of the flapper[,]" the 1920s saw "the explosion of African American art and culture now known as the Harlem Renaissance."

(D) is incorrect. The passage does not indicate that flappers and African American musicians worked together, only that they both used jazz music as a way to express themselves.

23. (A) is incorrect. Tough Alfie does not remember what happened, the phrase "doesn't remember anything between the referee's whistle and the thunderous roar of the crowd" indicates that he was able to take the shot.

(B) is incorrect. The crowd "expected perfection from him [Alfie,]" so the reader can imply that the "thunderous roar" was a result of a successful goal.

(C) is correct. The crowd's support for Alfie and their collective roar after the shot implies that Alfie scored the goal and won the championship.

(D) is incorrect. The crowd "expected perfection from him [Alfie]," so the reader can imply that the "thunderous roar" was a result of a successful goal and a winning performance.

24. (A) is incorrect. In regional studies, geographers "examine the characteristics of a particular place[.]"

(B) is incorrect. In topical studies, geographers "look at a single physical or human feature that impacts the world[.]"

(C) is incorrect. In physical studies, geographers "focus on the physical features of Earth[.]"

(D) is correct. The passage describes human studies as the study of "the relationship between human activity and the environment," which would include farmers interacting with river systems.

25. **(A) is correct.** A company that profits from private tutoring might introduce bias into a study on the effects of private tutoring in schools.

(B) is incorrect. A study showing the differences in standardized test scores between students in different neighborhoods would likely strengthen the author's argument by reinforcing the conclusion that private tutoring leads to educational inequality.

(C) is incorrect. Statements from local teachers would not weaken the author's argument about educational inequality because they are subjective and would not ensure equal opportunity.

(D) is incorrect. The study is not focused on college success.

MECHANICAL COMPREHENSION

1. **(C) is correct.** The gear that will mesh with Gear C needs to have the opposite orientation and be similar in size. The only gear that meets these conditions is Gear E.

2. **(C) is correct.** The height of the balls will change when the speed of the shaft changes (a higher speed will lift the balls upward). Since the speed has not changed, the balls will stay at the same level.

3. **(B) is correct.** The overall momentum of the system must be conserved. The product of force and distance for the woman will be equal to the raft but in the opposite direction (left).

   $140(10) = 700(d)$

   $d = \frac{1400}{700} = $ **2 ft. to the left**

4. **(B) is correct.** The larger the radius of a pulley, the slower it will turn. Because Pulley C has the largest radius, it will turn the slowest.

5. **(B) is correct.** If a lever's load is between the fulcrum and the effort, it is a second-class lever.

6. **(A) is correct.** The tension in the string keeps the ball rotating in a circle. When this force is removed, the ball will continue in the direction it was moving at that moment. The ball will move to the left.

7. **(B) is correct.** Blocks A and B will experience the same acceleration while they are on the incline. Both blocks will have a greater acceleration than C because gravity is increasing the net force moving the blocks down the incline.

8. **(A) is correct.** The product of teeth and revolutions will be equal for both gears.

   $12(2) = 24(r)$

   $r = \frac{24}{24} = $ **1 revolution**

9. **(B) is correct.** Steel is a conductor, and wood is an insulator, so the steel object will feel colder. The transfer of heat that makes the ball feel cold occurs because of conductivity, not because of density.

10. **(C) is correct.** When the ropes in the pulleys are crossed, adjacent pulleys rotate in opposite directions. Pulley B is in the middle, so it will be rotating in the opposite direction of the other two pulleys.

11. **(B) is correct.** The closer the string is to the center of the pulley, the faster the pulley rotates. Pulleys A and C are the same size, but the string is on the outer edge of Pulley A, so it will rotate slower than both C and B.

12. **(B) is correct.** Adjacent gears rotate in opposite directions, so Gears 2 and 4 will rotate in the opposite direction of Gear 3.

13. **(C) is correct.** The total force on each of the blocks is the same, so the block with the most springs will have the smallest force per spring. Block B's spring will experience the greatest force, then Block A's, and then Block C's.

14. **(B) is correct.** The screw will hit the contact point for each bump in the cam, so the screw will hit the contact point twice per turn. There are

two turns, so the screw will hit the contact point a total of four times.

15. **(A) is correct.** The product of the number of teeth and the revolutions for each gear will be equal.

$15(20)=10(r)$

$r = \frac{300}{10} = $ **30 revolutions**

16. **(A) is correct.** Adjacent gears rotate in opposite directions. Shafts B and C will rotate opposite of Shaft A. Shafts D and E will rotate in the opposite direction of Shaft C, which is the same direction as Shaft A.

17. **(B) is correct.** Each rotation of the arm rotates the disc to the next slot. This disc rotates a third of a turn for each rotation of the arm. If the arm turns three times, the disc performs one complete turn.

18. **(B) is correct.** An object traveling in an arc has a velocity of zero at the top of its path and is moving slower the closer it is to that point. The object will also have the same speed at both points on the path that have the same height. So, the ball will be moving the fastest at points A and E, since both have the same height and are farthest from the top of the arc.

19. **(C) is correct.** The two charges are both negative, so they will repel each other and move apart.

20. **(A) is correct.**

Plug in the values for each resistor. Calculate the equivalent resistance.

$\frac{1}{R_{eq}} = \frac{1}{R_1} + \frac{1}{R_2} + ... + \frac{1}{R_n}$

$\frac{1}{R_{eq}} = \frac{1}{1\ k\Omega} + \frac{1}{2\ k\Omega} + \frac{1}{0.5\ k\Omega} = 3.5\frac{1}{k\Omega}$

$R_{eq} = $ **0.3 kΩ**

21. **(B) is correct.**

Plug in the values for current and resistance to get the voltage.

$V = IR$

$V = 0.001\ A \times 1000\ \Omega = $ **1 V**

22. **(C) is correct.** The largest mass will be the hardest to move. The space station has the largest mass.

23. (A) is incorrect. The tension will be equal to the weight it supports, 100 N.

(B) is incorrect. The tension will be equal to the weight it supports, 100 N.

(C) is correct. The tension will be equal to the weight it supports, 100 N.

24. **(B) is correct.** The screw will hit the contact point for each bump in the cam, so the screw will hit the contact point twice per turn. There are two turns, so the screw will hit the contact point a total of four times.

25. **(B) is correct.** There are 4 threads per inch on the bolt.